CW01239303

MUHAMMAD
ﷺ

Encyclopaedia of Seerah

FOR CHILDREN
volume one

LIFE-STYLE

OH! PROPHET OF ALLAH

I wish to say someday soon, Oh! Prophet of Allah:
I love thee more times than the stars in the sky.
I love thee more times than the rays of the sun.
I love thee more times than the grains of sand in a desert.
I love thee more times than the clouds in the sky.
I love thee more times than rain drops all over the world.
I love thee more than the scorched earth loveth water.
My love for you is greater than the greatest of mountains,
My love is mightier than the sea,
And if I had a thousand, million lifetimes I would prove this to thee.

Ahmad Naeem Azar (student)

Editorial Board
Afzalur Rahman
Col. Dr. Yusuf Abbasi
Prof. Muhammad Yusuf
Yasmin Hassan

SEERAH FOUNDATION
LONDON

© SEERAH FOUNDATION
MUHAMMAD (Ⓟ) ENCYCLOPAEDIA OF SEERAH
For Children
Volume 1

ISBN Hardback 0 907052 50 9

British Library Cataloguing in Publication Data

FIRST EDITION: MAY, 1994

Produced and distributed by:
Seerah Foundation,
78 Gillespie Road, London N5 1LN

Designed by Xheight Limited.
Printed in England by Halstan & Co. Ltd.,
Plantation Road,
Amersham,
Bucks HP6 6HJ U.K.

Arabia: The Land of Muhammad's Birth

The Arabian Peninsula lies to the east of Africa. It is bordered to the north by Palestine and Syria; Iraq and Iran to the east; the Gulf of Aden and the Arabian Sea to the south; and the Red Sea to the west.

The Arabian Peninsula is about 1400 miles in length and 1250 miles in breadth and it has an area of about one million square miles.

The Arabian Peninsula, in general, may be described as a plateau. It is remarkable for its barrenness and dryness. Mainly it is a desert country, with numerous widely scattered oases in the dry valleys. It receives scant rainfall on rare occasions.

Thus the way of life in the Arabian Peninsula was generally nomadic. And the desert tribes continually moved around in the desert in search of water and food.

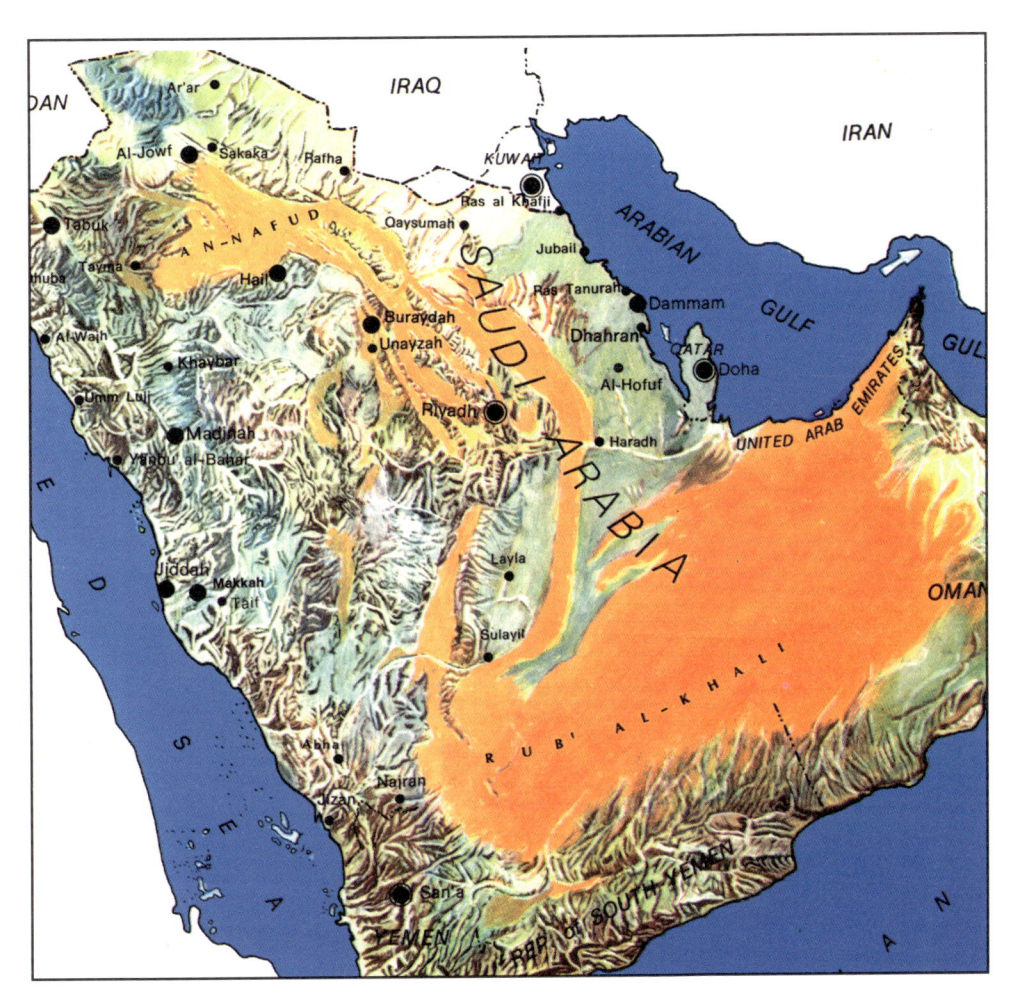

Map of Arabia.

In full flood, these valleys become violent rivers. And of the major cities of Arabia, few have been so affected by the consequences of flooding in the past as Makkah, in the foothills of the Hejaz. Since early times the Ka'bah itself has been occasionally engulfed by flood water.

Climate: The entire Red Sea coast normally has a sub-tropical climate. Typical of this climate are warm summers with a very high percentage of humidity. The winters are moderate and have light rains in the months of November through February.

In ancient times only the coastal areas came into contact with the civilised world, while the rest of Arabia was completely unknown.

Tribal disputes were common among the desert people. The Arabs had no central government and lived mostly a nomadic life. They fought one another endlessly over meagre supplies of water and scanty pasture. And they were never united before Islam. Thus in a political sense they had practically no influence at all. The Romans and the Persians treated the Arabs as their subjects although none of them had ever occupied their land or attacked them.

The Holy Ka'bah at dusk.

The Arab people and the Holy Ka'bah

The Arabs are either descendants of Banu Qahtan or Banu Isma'il; the former are descendants of Eber mentioned in the Bible, Genesis, Chapter X, while the latter are children of Isma'il, the eldest son of the Prophet Ibrahim (Abraham) by Hagar, the Egyptian lady. The Prophet Ibrahim was born in Ur, the capital of the Babalonian kings, but was forced to leave his native land, Iraq, because of his dislike for the idolatrous practices and beliefs of his parents and his people. He left his country with his nephew, Lut, who also believed in his Monotheistic religion.

The Great Mosque in Makkah.

Isma'il was born to his second wife, Hagar. The Qur'an mentions the glad tidings of the birth of his second son Ishaque to his first wife Sarah when his eldest son Isma'il had almost reached puberty (51:28-30). The descendants of Isma'il came to be known as the Arabs who settled in the Arabian Peninsula and the descendants of Ishaque came to be known as the children of Israel who lived in Palestine.

Land of Prophet Muhammad.

Building of the Ka'bah

The first Holy Mosque, the Ka'bah, in Makkah was built by Adam. It was destroyed by the Great Flood in the time of the Prophet Nuh. The Prophets Ibrahim and his son, Isma'il, were ordered by Allah to rebuild it on its old foundations. So Ibrahim and Isma'il together built this Holy House in Makkah. Since then it has been revered as a Holy place.

Aerial view of the Holy Ka'bah and Makkah.

Ka'bah, after extension, 1894-1994. The block on the left is a recent addition.

Holy Ka'bah is the (Qibla) – the direction in which all Muslims of the world turn in prayer five times a day. It is the only spot on earth where worship never ceases. It continues round the clock.

On the occasion of pilgrimage the greatest congregation of the world is held round it. It is estimated that more than two and a half million Muslims perform pilgrimage every year and an equal number visit it to perform the umra.

The site of Ka'bah which was established by Allah has always been regarded as sacred and most holy by the followers of the religion of the Prophet Ibrahim even before the coming of the Prophet Muhammad (ⓓ).

Perhaps the covering (Kiswah) of the Ka'bah is the most important sign of care and honour for the Holy House. It is narrated that the Holy Mosque (Ka'bah) has been adorned with a cover since the time of the Prophet Isma'il. The Prophet Muhammad (ⓓ) is reported to have made a covering of Yemenite cloth.

The Door of the Ka'bah

The door of the Ka'bah is raised above the ground, about eleven and a half spans. The door has two large silver staples on which is hung the lock.

Door of the Ka'bah.

About 520 A.D., Abraha, the Christian ruler of the Abyssinian Kingdom of Yemen, led an expedition to destroy Ka'bah in Makkah. But his army, including hundreds of elephants, perished near Makkah and no one survived from his troops.

The Qur'an refers to this event in these words: (105:1-5).

Have you not seen how your Lord dealt with the companions of the elephant? Did He not cause their plan to end in confusion? And sent against them birds in flocks casting at them stones of baked clay.

So He rendered them like straw eaten up?

The side view of the Holy Ka'bah during pilgrimage.

The Prophet Muhammad (ﷺ) Life at Makkah

The last Prophet, Muhammad (ﷺ) was born in Arabia at a time when the message of the previous Messengers of Allah had been lost and mankind was groping its way through the darkness of ignorance. The Arabs had forgotten the religion of their forefathers, Ibrahim and Isma'il (ﷺ) and had started worshipping idols and stones in the House of Allah, the Ka'bah. The teachings of Moses and Jesus (ﷺ) were practically lost by their followers. They had changed and corrupted the teachings of Allah's Messengers and mixed other ideas with them. The doctrine of monotheism had lost its practical significance and implications both for the Jews and the Christians, while the Arabs were engulfed in the worship of idols and polytheism. The Last Messenger of Allah was born when the whole world had forgotten the Message of the Creator and was lost in the wilderness of polytheism.

The house where the Prophet was born. It lies to the north east of the Holy Ka'bah. Now it is used as a library.

The army of Abraha is said to have perished somewhere in this valley between Arafat and Mina.

The Prophet's city of birth and the holy Ka'bah

The Prophet Muhammad (ﷺ) was born in Makkah, Arabia (now called Saudi Arabia) on Monday, 12th. Rabi'al-Awwal (2nd. August, 570 A.D.) to the noble family of Bani Hashim, of the Quraish.

The city of Makkah was the centre for devotion to the Ka'bah, the Holy House of prayer built by the Prophet Ibrahim and his son Isma'il, through whom Arabs claim their ancestry.

Makkah is set in a rugged landscape consisting mostly of solid granite, with rocks sometimes reaching 300 metres above sea level. It is enclosed by the valley of Ibrahim, which is surrounded by mountain ranges to the east, west and south. Its climate is dry and hot with temperatures ranging from 15 degrees in winter to 45 degrees in summer.

The Holy Ka'bah was rebuilt on several occasions in the pre-Islamic period of Jahiliyyah, by Qusayyb b.Kilab, an ancestor of the Prophet Muhammad (ﷺ), and again in the days of A'bd-al-Muttalib, the grandfather of the Prophet. Yet another rebuilding took place not long before the coming of Islam, as a result of flooding, a major problem of the city until very recent times. The Holy Ka'bah at this time was 18 cubits high and the level rested on 6 columns. The Black Stone was put in place by the Prophet Muhammad (ﷺ) himself, assisted by the chiefs of the Quraish.

The Black Stone (Hajr-i-Aswad) is in the same position today, marking the starting point of Tawaf.

Childhood

Muhammad (ﷺ) was born an orphan. His father had died before his birth. According to the tradition of the noble families of Makkah, he was taken by a foster mother, Halimah, to her village, where he lived for a few years in the care of his foster parents.

He was brought home a number of times to visit his mother in Makkah. The boy was returned to his mother when he was about four or five years old.

His mother, Amina, took her little son to Madinah for visiting relatives and seeing the grave of his father. On the return journey to Makkah, she died on the way. Muhammad (ﷺ) was left alone. He was brought back to Makkah by a slave girl named Umm-i-Aiyman.

Bedouin boy on the Arabian Peninsula driving his flock of sheep.

After the death of his mother, his grandfather Abd al Muttalib, took custody of the child but it was not long before his grandfather died too. Muhammad (ﷺ) was then eight years old. Now his uncle, Abu Talib, took care of him and became his guardian.

At the age of ten or twelve he tended flocks of sheep. According to Abu Hurairah, the Messenger said, "Allah did not raise any prophet but as a shepherd." His companions asked him "Did you do the same?" "Yes, I used to shepherd the sheep of the people of Makkah for some qirats." It was a common profession for boys of that age in Arabia in those times to tend the sheep and goats. The Prophet was no exception. Before Muhammad, Moses, Jesus and David did the same.

A view of the city of Makkah with Ka'bah in the forefront.

One of the main gates of Ka'bah.

Muhammad (ﷺ) was a thoughtful and hardworking boy. Neither was he noisy nor naughty and rude. Gladly he did little chores for the elders. Not a glum, cheerless child, he was calm and a well-mannered boy.

Abu Talib, his uncle, was very kind to him and brought him up as his own son. Muhammad (ﷺ) was also greatly attached to his uncle and lived quite happily with him. When he was twelve, he accompanied his uncle on a trading trip to Syria. It was during this journey that a Christian monk known as Bahirah told his uncle that the boy would be a Prophet of Allah and advised him to return to his country and take care of his nephew.

Youth

Muhammad (ﷺ) was a very hard working young man, who was ready to do any honest work to earn his living. He learned trading from his uncle and became a trader. First he went with his uncle on commercial trips and later he began to trade on his own. He was extremely honest and fair in his dealings. He lived a very quiet and peaceful life and was respected and honoured by the people of Makkah, rich as well as poor.

In his youth, he was a firm believer in one Allah and hated polytheism and stayed away fom idol worship.

He was a handsome young man and people of all shades of opinion respected and honoured him and thoroughly trusted him.

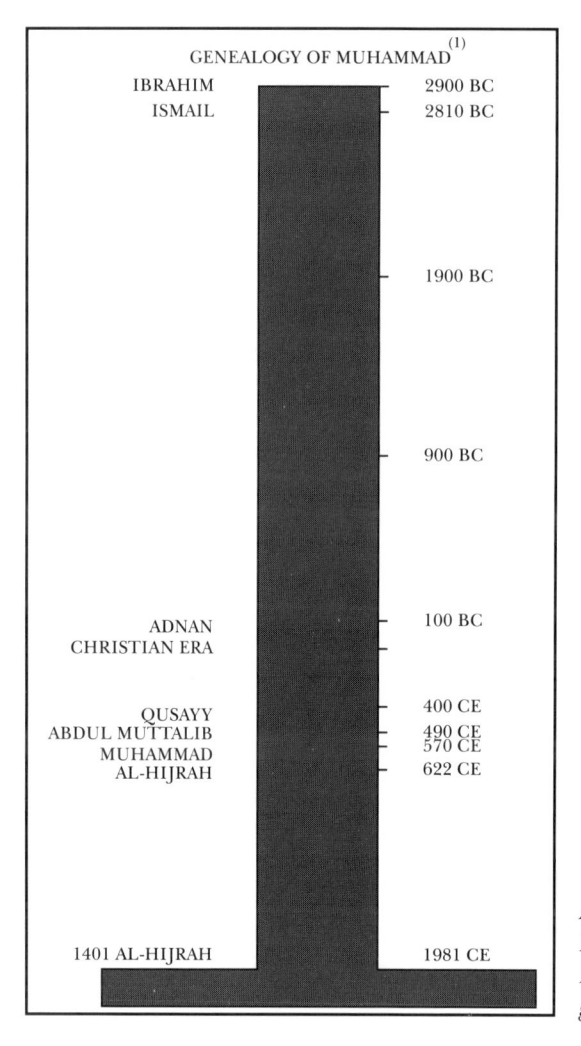

GENEALOGY OF MUHAMMAD [1]

IBRAHIM	2900 BC
ISMAIL	2810 BC
	1900 BC
	900 BC
ADNAN	100 BC
CHRISTIAN ERA	
QUSAYY	400 CE
ABDUL MUTTALIB	490 CE
MUHAMMAD	570 CE
AL-HIJRAH	622 CE
1401 AL-HIJRAH	1981 CE

According to Ibn Abbas, Allah's Prophet never went beyond Ma'add bin Adnan in his genealogy.

An upright youth of spotless character who had earned the respect and trust of the people. Warm and loving to his friends; generous and helpful to the poor and sympathetic to the needy.

He was truthful and considerate to all. He honoured his promises and trusts to his friends and foes alike. He was intelligent and wise and was not touched by anger.

He lived a poor and simple life. He was humble but confident and hated vanity and pride. He shared the pains and sufferings of the poor, widows and orphans. He abstained from gambling, drinking, vulgar wrangling and other vices common among young people. He greatly impressed the people of Makkah by his spotless character and was commonly known as as-Sadiq (the truthful) and al-Amin (the trustworthy).

The Curtain of the Holy Ka'bah Door. The inscribed curtain was first hung on the door of the Holy Ka'bah in 810 H/1407 AD., and it has continued to be hung until now.

The Covenant of Al-Fadhul

As a young man, he actively participated in forming a confederacy among the tribes of Makkah, for maintaining peace. Makkans were tired and sick of inter-tribal fighting and bloodshed. At last it was decided to maintain peace, suppress violence and injustice and uphold the rights of the poor, the destitute and weak. An oath was taken to keep peace, and it was called the Covenant (agreement) of Al-Fadhul. Muhammad (ﷺ) was one of the peacemakers.

The Covenant must have been formed somewhere around the Ka'bah, in the centre of this picture.

Building of the Ka'bah

The Ka'bah is situated at the lowest point in the valley of Faran and is always flooded by rain water. The people of Makkah tried various methods to stop this rainwater flooding the Ka'bah, but all their attempts failed and the building was damaged by floods. The people of Makkah, therefore, decided to rebuild it. The different parts of the building were divided among the leading families of Makkah and work was completed in harmony and without any dispute until the time came to install the Black Stone (Hajr-i-Aswad) at its proper place. Then a dispute arose among the chiefs of Makkah. Everyone wanted the honour of putting the Holy Stone in its proper place. There was fear of possible bloodshed over this important issue but a proposal from an old wise man was accepted by all and saved the situation. He proposed that he who entered the Ka'bah first of all on the following morning should decide the issue.

The city of Makkah, Ka'bah is in the centre of the city.

The Ka'bah in 1890. Probably the Makkan chiefs were arguing about the placing of the Black Stone (Hajr-i-Aswad) on this side of the Ka'bah in this picture.

It so happened that Muhammad (D) was the first person to enter Ka'bah next morning. When the people saw him entering the House of Allah, they were very pleased and shouted with one voice: "Here comes Al-Amin! Here comes Al-Amin!" They all declared that they were quite willing to accept the decision of Muhammad (D). Muhammad (D) took a very wise decision in this respect. He asked the leaders of the different families of Quraish to hold the four corners of a sheet of cloth which he spread on the ground.

He placed the Black Stone in the middle of the sheet and asked them all to lift it up together. When the sheet reached the proper height, he lifted the Black Stone and laid it in its proper place with his own hands.

Thus an ugly situation was saved and problem resolved amicably by the wisdom and foresight of Muhammad (ﷺ) in his youth. And at the same time, Allah got placed the Holy Stone in its proper position with the hands of His Last Messenger on earth and the Polytheists of Makkah were deprived of this great honour by their own decision.

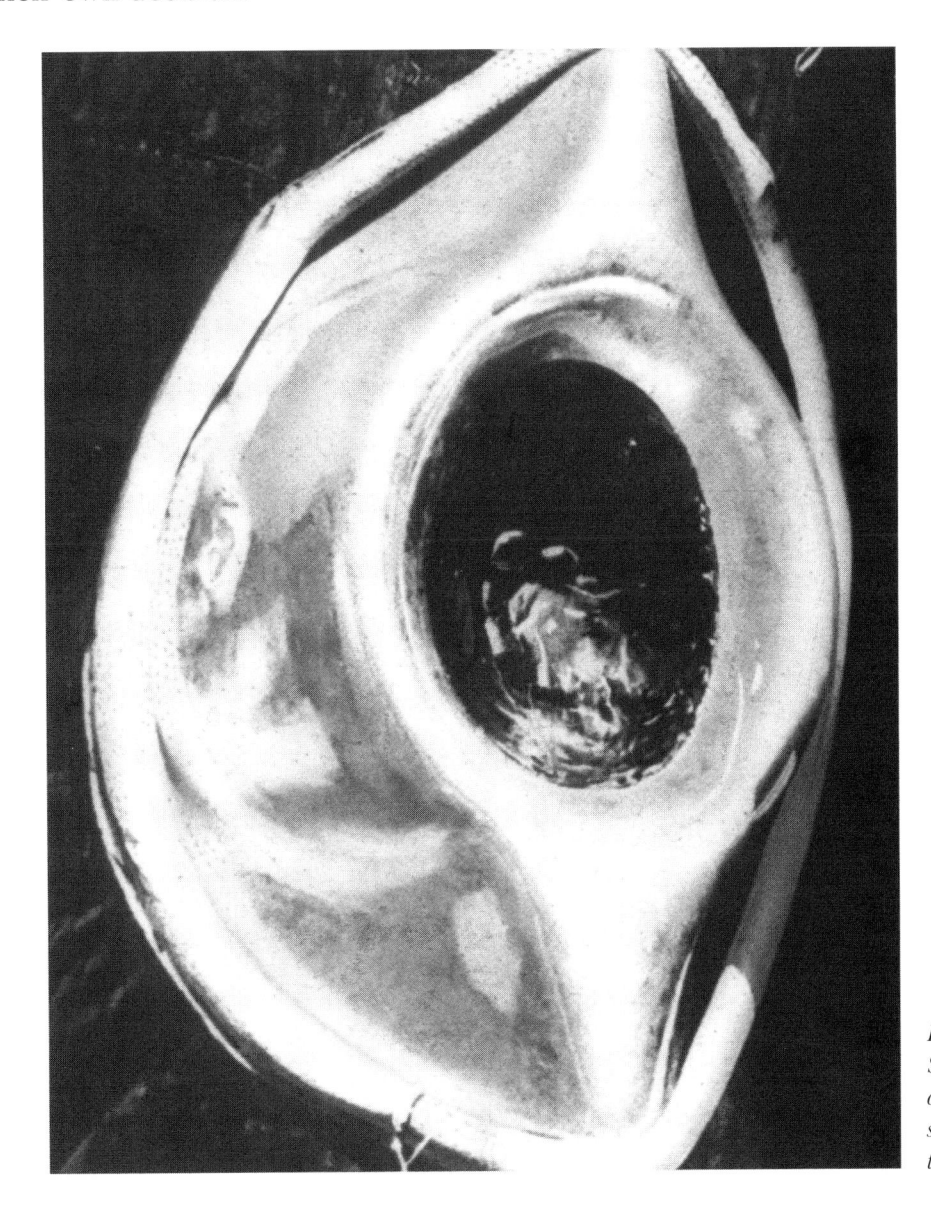

Hajr-i-Aswad (The Black Stone), is in the south-east corner of the Ka'bah. It is set in a silver frame in this corner of the Ka'bah.

Maqam-i-Ibrahim

On one side of The Holy Ka'bah there stands a round crystal case which contains a piece of stone. This stone bears a footprint of Prophet Ibrahim. It is called Maqam-i-Ibrahim and is mentioned in the Qur'an in these words: "Indeed the First House of worship ever to be built for mankind is the one which is at Bakkah (i.e., Makkah). (It was) blessed (and made the Centre of) Guidance for all peoples. In it are clear signs: (It is) the Place (of Worship) of Ibrahim and whoever enters it is safe and secure." (3:96-9).

After the completion of Tawaf (circumambulation), two rakah prayers are offered behind the station of Ibrahim. It is narrated that Prophet Ibrahim stood on this stone when he was building the Ka'bah. The stone still bears the footprint of Prophet Ibrahim.

Maqam-i-Ibrahim In Ka'bah.

Manhood

As he grew older, Muhammad's (ⓓ) qualities of goodness and righteousness became well-known to his friends and fellow citizens of Makkah and its suburbs. His reputation as an honest and virtuous man was well established beyond doubt. The people of Makkah respected him and they left their valuables in his safe keeping.

His reputation grew but he was sick of the corrupt society around him. He was pained to see people make idols of stone and wood and then to worship them as gods. It made him sad to see the cruelty of man to man and to animals.

He used to go away from Makkah, and spent days and nights, in a cave, on top of mount Hira (now called Mount of Light, Jabal-i-Nur), lost in prayers and deep thought.

Jabal-i-Nur.

Marriage

He was 25 years old and well-known in Makkah as an honest, pious and virtuous trader. He helped the poor and the widows and loved the orphans and weak. A wealthy and respectable widow, Khadijah bint Khuwailid, was very much impressed by his pleasing personality and character. She was forty years old and twice widowed. She had two sons and a daughter and quite a fortune from her two husbands. She offered herself in marriage and Muhammad (ⓓ) accepted her.

They were married and enjoyed a happy, successful and peaceful married life for many years and had two sons, both of whom died in childhood, and four daughters. Khadijah was the Prophet's only wife as long as she lived. She died when he was about 51 years old.

He married ten times after the death of Khadijah and all his wives, excepting A'ishah, were either widows or divorced. Some of them he married to help the widows of his companions. Some were accepted to win over the support of hostile tribes or to honour the head of the tribe. He treated all his wives with love, kindness and fairness.

The City of Makkah with the Holy Mosque, Ka'bah.

Search for Truth

All these years, Muhammad (ﷺ) tried hard to search for the Truth. He was disturbed by the appalling misery and evils of his time. His wife gave him support in his efforts to find a way out of the prevailing darkness of evil and idolatory. He often took food with him to the mountain of Hira and stayed there for days. His wife sent more food to him there.

His mind revolted against the pagan gods and goddesses of Makkah. Often he wondered and thought of the God of his forefathers, Ibrahim and Isma'il. His search for truth in the wilderness of idolatory is described in the Qur'an in these words, "And He found you wandering, and gave you guidance." (93:7).

Muhammad (ﷺ) was born in the midst of idolatory (idol worship) and his family was the custodian of the Ka'bah which was then full of idols. He wandered around in search of the monotheism (One God) of his ancestors. At last he found the guidance of Allah on the mount of Hira.

TRANSLATION: You are indeed one of the messengers, on a straight way (From your Lord). (The Qur'an).

Prophethood

As usual, one day he was at the (cave) of Hira, when the angel Gabriel came to him and asked him to read. It was so sudden and unexpected that he was startled by the voice in that calm and quiet atmosphere of the cave. He paused, and then answered, "I cannot read." The angel repeated his request and he gave the same answer. The third time the angel said, "Read! In the name of your Lord who created – created man from a clot! and your Lord is most Bountiful, Who taught by means of the pen, taught man that which he knew not." (96:1-5).

This was the first Revelation and the beginning of the Prophethood of Muhammad (Ⓓ). He was then forty years old.

*The First Revelation
The Qur'an : 96
(Surah Al-Alaq).*

He came home, astonished and shaken. The Appearance of the angel and his selection for this great mission was rather astounding. He told the whole story to his wife. She comforted him and assured him that no harm could come to a man of his nature and that Allah would protect him from all evil. She took him to her cousin, Warqa bin Naufal, who was a scholarly person and had embraced Christianity. After hearing from Muhammad (ﷺ) what had happened on the mount Hira, he said that that was the Angel Gabriel, who had always brought revelation to the Messengers from Allah before him. He also said that the Prophet would be turned out of his city by his enemies. He further added that he would certainly support him. After an interval, the Revelations continued and Muhammad (ﷺ) quietly, but steadfastly, began to preach the Message of Islam (Oneness of God): The rights of man – between men and women, parents, relatives, neighbours, and others. His wife Khadijah was the first to embrace Islam. Then his close associates, one by one, began to come into the fold of Islam. His very close friend Abu Bakr, his slave Zaid, his cousin Ali, and then Othman bin Uffan, Talha, Zubair and Abdur Rahman bin Auf became Muslims.

View from the Cave in Mount Hira. A favoured retreat of Muhammad's in the hills, a few miles from his home.

Muhammad (☮) continued to preach Oneness of Allah (Tawhid) in secret for three years. Then God commanded him to preach the religion of Islam (Submission to Allah and peace) openly to his kinsmen: "Therefore expound openly what you are commanded, and turn away from those who join false gods with Allah." (15:94).

And in Surah Al-Shu'ara we read, "So, call not on any other god with Allah, or you will be among those under the penalty. And admonish your nearest kinsmen." (26:213-214).

Muhammad (☮) gathered his kinsmen by the mount of safa and addressed them: "Would you believe me, if I tell you that an army is on the other side of the hill to attack you?" They said in one voice, "We shall believe you. You have always been truthful." He said "Then believe me, Allah (Your God) is One. Let no other god stand with Allah." On hearing this, they flew into a rage and asked how could they give up the gods worshiped by their forefathers? They turned against him and mocked him. Then they dispersed and left him alone on the hill.

The Running (Sa'i) between Safa and Marwah. (The people of Quraish must have assembled somewhere on this side of the picture near mount Safa to listen to the Prophet).

28

A piece of Kiswah, the hand-embroidered cloth, decorated with verses from the Qur'an, which adorns the Ka'bah: It is narrated that the Prophet Isma'il made a cover for the Ka'bah. Some say that Adnan Ibn Add the top ancestor of the Prophet was the first to cover the Ka'bah.

He continued preaching, in spite of hostility and abuses from the leaders of Makkah, especially from his uncle, Abu Lahab. Some leading men of his tribe, the Quraish, but mostly the poor, the weak and slaves, came into the fold of Islam, in spite of increasing hostility from the pagans of Makkah.

But the poor and the weak converts to Islam, like Bilal, a negro slave, Ammar bin Yasir, Khabbab and others like them, suffered torture and severe persecution at the hands of the chiefs of Makkah.

However, opposition to Muhammad's (ﷺ) mission kept on growing in its fury and harshness, thorns were strewn in his way, garbage heaped on him and foul abuses hurled at him but he continued his work with increasing vigour and determination.

Migration to Abyssinia (Hijrah)

As the persecution and torture of the Messenger of Allah and his followers intensified, about eighty Muslims were allowed to emigrate to the neighbouring friendly Abyssinia. It was then ruled by a gentle and trustworthy Christian King called Negus (Najashi), who afterwards embraced Islam. Some years later his uncle, Hamza and Umar bin Khattab, great warriors and eminent leaders of the Quraish, became Muslims. Their conversion to Islam encouraged Muslims to pray publicly in the Ka'bah. The chiefs of the Quraish were now alarmed and they all joined together to crush this movement by force.

Jabal-i-Thaur, about ten kilometres from Makkah.

Boycott

When the Quraish found that their threats, persecution and torture of Muhammad (ⓓ) and his followers had no real effect and the number of Muslims was slowly and steadily increasing, they asked his uncle Abu Talib, to hand him over to them. When he refused, the Makkan chiefs, decided to boycott the Banu Hashim (the family of the Prophet). The Banu Hashim had to take refuge in Shu'b Abi Talib (now called Shu'b Ali) near a hillock quite close to the Ka'bah. They suffered for three years and had to live very often without food and water for days. This boycott lasted from the seventh year to the tenth year of the Prophethood.

During the boycott the family of the Prophet (Banu Hashim) took refuge in Shu'b Abi Talib (now called Shu'b Ali).

Loss of Two Friends

Just after the end of the boycott, Muhammad (ⓓ) lost his most affectionate uncle, and faithful and loving wife Khadijah.

These tragic losses in one year left him without love and support of dear ones. In the meantime misery and suffering of Muslims had become unbearable.

In the same year Muhammad (ⓓ) went to Taif, a hill resort about thirty miles from Makkah, to take the Divine Message to its people. He was mercilessly attacked and stoned by them. He was so badly hurt that he almost fainted there and blood from his wounds filled his shoes. But he wished them no ill. When asked to curse his tormentors, he forgave them and prayed that Allah might bring them and their children to the path of Islam.

General view of Taif City.

The wicked people of Taif hooted him through the streets and threw stones at him. And while he was trying to leave the city, some rogues pursued him to the edge of the city. Zaid, his freed slave, who was trying to shield him, was also wounded in the head. The mob did not rest until they had chased him a few miles from the city. Muhammad (Ⓓ) wounded, wearied and exhausted, took refuge in one of the many orchards around Taif. There he rested against the wall of a vineyard.

The Holy Mosque in 1984. Angel Gabriel appeared one night while Muhammad (Ⓓ) was sleeping in the house of Umm Hani, daughter of Abu Talib. Then he took him with him and showed the marvels of Allah's creation. Umm Hani's house used to be somewhere in the corner of the new building on the right side of Ka'bah in this picture.

Ascension (Mi'raj)

During those difficult days, he was bestowed with a divine favour. This event commonly known as Mi'raj (Ascension) is mentioned in Surah Al-Isra' in these words,

"Glory to Allah, Who did take His servant for a journey in a part of the night from the sacred Mosque (Ka'bah) to the farthest Mosque (Al-Aqsa) whose surroundings We did bless, in order that We might show him some of our Signs." (17:1).

One night Muhammad (ⓓ) was taken by the angel Gabriel to the Mosque Al-Aqsa in Jerusalem and from there to the World of Allah and was shown the mysteries and miracles of the universe. This was in fact, a sign that he was the last Messenger of Allah and that His Message would remain for ever to guide mankind until the Day of Resurrection.

Another view of Shi'b Ali and the House of the Prophet, bottom left corner.

Covenant of Aqabah (Bai'at Aqabah)

In the eleventh year of his mission six men came from Madinah for the pilgrimage and saw the Prophet (☉). They embraced Islam and the next year twelve pilgrims came to Makkah and embraced Islam and swore, "We will not worship any deity but Allah, We will neither steal, nor commit adultery, nor kill our children. We will obey the Messenger of Allah in all that is good." This is known as the First Covenant of Aqabah.

The people of Madinah probably took the pledge somewhere here between Mina and Arafat during the pilgrimage.

The next year, in the thirteenth year of the Prophethood, 73 men and 2 women came for the pilgrimage from Madinah. When they learned that the Prophet (ⓓ) was thinking of leaving Makkah, they invited him to Madinah and pledged full support to him, his mission and his followers. They took the pledge in these words, "We will all obey you, O Messenger of Allah, in all circumstances, in plenty and in scarcity, in joy and in sorrow, and we will not wrong anyone. We will speak the truth at all times, and we will fear the censure of none in the service of Allah."

The Holy Mosque and the Honourable Ka'bah.

Emigration to Madinah (Hijrah)

By this time the Makkan leaders had become desperate and wanted to put an end to the whole affair. They decided to assassinate the Prophet one night and end his mission. The Prophet (ⓓ) was informed by the angel Gabriel of the plan of his enemies and was told to leave Makkah that very night.

A group of Muslims crossed the Red Sea on their way to Abyssinia. (The first migrants.)

The Prophet (ﷺ) asked 'Ali to stay in his bed to pay back the valuables entrusted to him by various people and quietly left the house, unnoticed by anyone.

Hijrah (Migration)

In the thirteenth year of the Prophethood, Muhammad (ﷺ) on direction from His Lord, one night left his house while the Makkan youths who had surrounded his house lay unconscious in sleep. As had been arranged with Abu Bakr, they both went to the opposite direction of Madinah and hid themselves in the cave on the mountain of Thaur a few miles away from Makkah.

The Prophet stayed in the cave for three nights and on the fourth day left for Madinah. A reliable man was hired as a guide who

The Makkan youth at the door of the Prophet's house at night to assassinate him. The Prophet's house is on the right side in this picture. They must have stood on the other side of the house.

led the way. The news of the Prophet's arrival had reached Madinah. All the people of Madinah were anxiously waiting for him. The Prophet stayed in Quba about three miles from Madinah. After fourteen days stay in Quba, he left for the city of Madinah.

Enthusiasm of the people of Madinah ran so high that women appeared on the roofs of their houses and sang: "Full moon has risen on us, coming out of the valley of Wada', grateful to Allah, we ought to remain, so long as devotees live and pray."

And little girls played on their tambourines and sang: "We are the daughters of Banu Najjar, What a good neighbour we have in Muhammad (ⓓ)." Muhammad (ⓓ) asked them if they liked him. The girls answered that they did. Muhammad (ⓓ) replied, "I too like you."

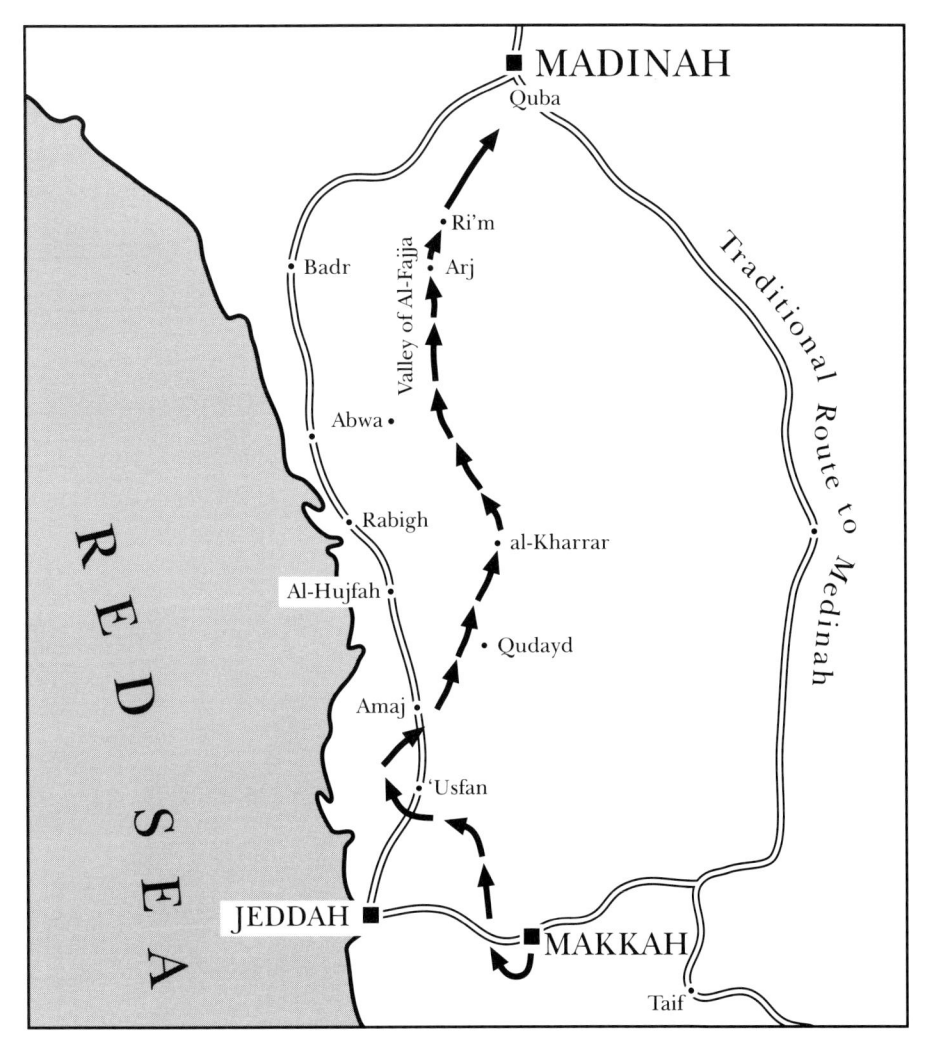

The route of Hijrah an-Nabwiah.

The Prophet stayed at Quba for 14 days and then went to Madinah. He built a mosque there which is called the Mosque of Quba. The Prophet himself worked with his Companions for the construction of this mosque. He carried stones on his back along with other people.

The Mosque of Quba.

When the Makkan chiefs found Ali in Muhammad's (D) bed next morning, they were furious and more determined than ever to find him. They offered a huge reward for his capture, dead or alive, but he and Abu Bakr reached Madinah safely.

This event is called Hijrah.

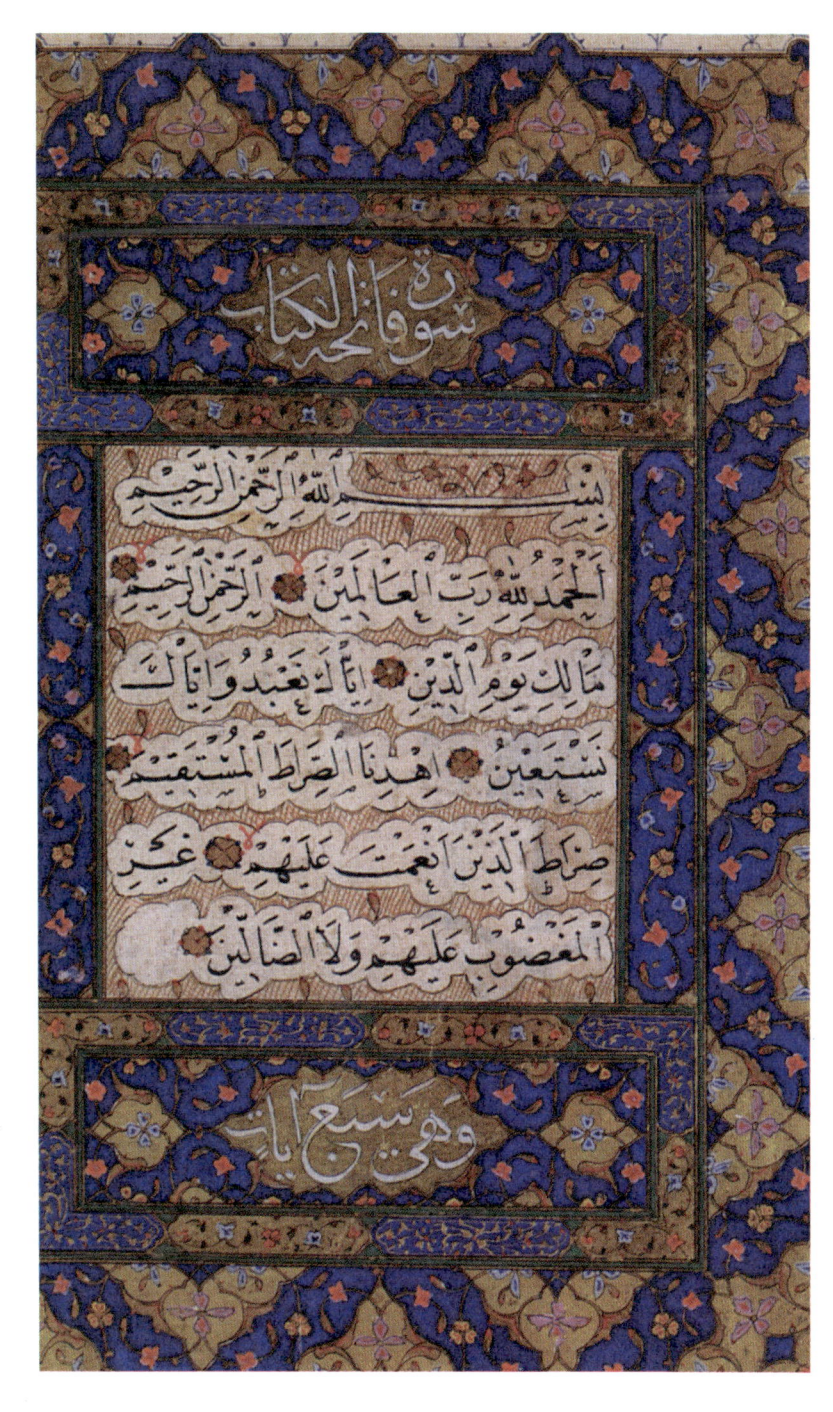

The first surah (chapter) of the Qur'an.

The Islamic Calendar

Later on, the year of Muhammad's (ⓓ) emigration (Hijrah) to Madinah was selected to mark the beginning of the Islamic Calendar. It began from the 1st of Muharram (lunar month) of the year of Hijrah, or 15th July, 622 A.C.

General view of the Prophet's Mosque.

The Hejaz and the City of Prophet's Hijrah (Migration)

The geography of Western Arabia is dominated by the Hejaz mountains. The northern part of the Hejaz is rugged and generally barren, and the mountains do not rise to a great height. In this desert land there are scattered oases in the otherwise harsh landscape.

The southern highlands enjoy a far cooler climate than the rest of the country. They receive frequent rainfall and mist even in summer. In the foothills, valleys carry the flood water from the Hejaz highlands westwards to the Tihama's coastal plain where they end in the desert. Although no perennial streams reach the Red Sea, flowing streams and pools can be seen in the foothills even in summer.

The next morning the Makkan chiefs found Ali in the Prophet's bed. The Prophet's house is on the right side in front of the main blocks of buildings in this picture.

Geography

The Land of Hejaz, which includes two of our holiest places, Makkah and Madinah, lies in the western coast of Saudi Arabia. The Red Sea separates the land of Hejaz from the main continent of Africa.

Along the Red Sea lies a narrow plain whose width varies from one place to another ranging from 40 miles to 30 miles and even less when it reaches the north. The coastal plain is characterised by extensive marshlands and lava fields.

East of this coastal plain runs a range of high mountains broken by great valleys, of which the most important are Wadi Al-Himdh, Wadi Yanbu and Wadi Fatimah. The highest mountains are in the northwest where peaks rise to over 9,000 feet. Then they fall to 8,000 feet to the west of Makkah, to 4,000 feet to the west of Mahd Adh-Dhahab and to 3,000 feet at Madinah.

Climate

The land of Hejaz normally has a sub-tropical climate. Typical of this climate are warm summers with very high humidity. The winters are moderate and have light rains in the months from November to February.

Madinah, the city of Prophet's Hijrah (Migration)

Madinah lies some 425 kilometres north of Jeddah, 497 kilometres from Makkah and to the east of the Red Sea; only about 250 kilometres away from it. It is surrounded by a number of mountains: Pilgrims' (Al-Hujaj) mountain to the west, Sala' to the north-west, Caravan (or Al-Eer) mountain to the south and Uhud to the north.

Madinah is situated on a flat plateau at the junction of the three valleys of Al-Aql, Al-Aqiq, and Al-Himdh. For this reason there are large green areas amidst a dry mountainous region. Madinah is rich

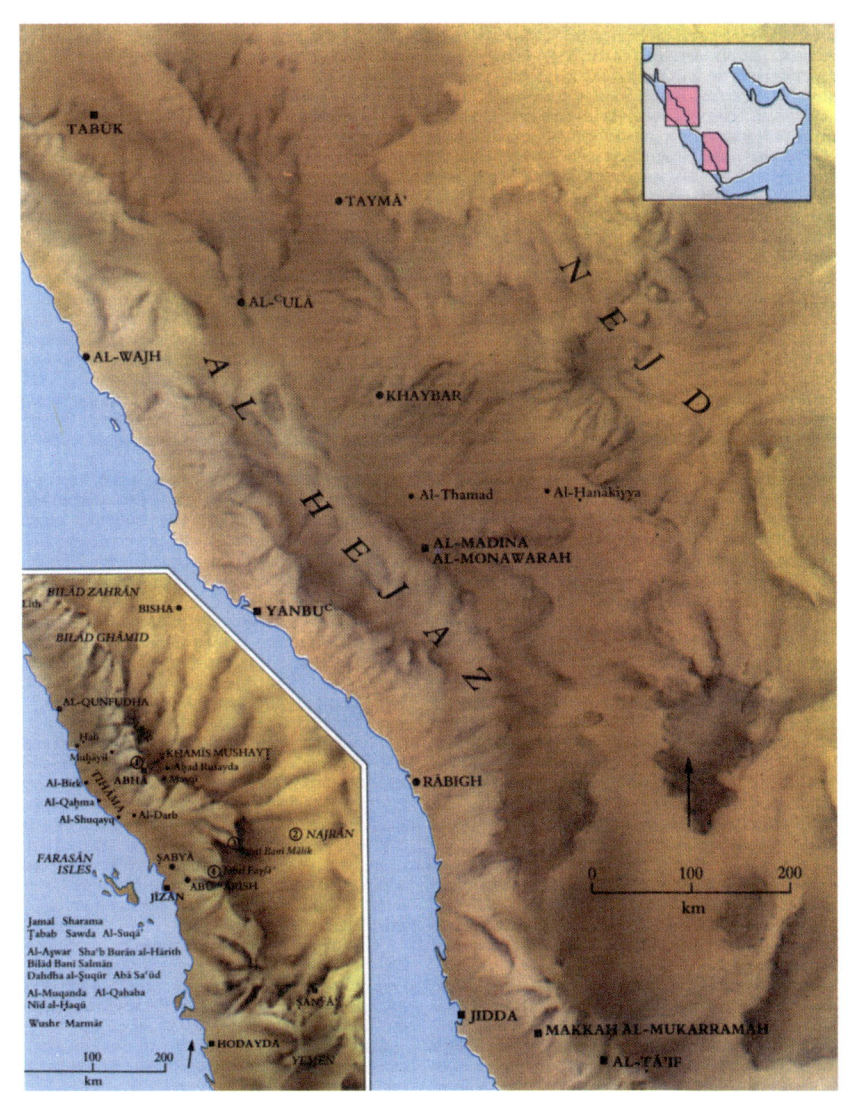

Map of Hejaz.

in water and agricultural products, especially dates. It is 620 metres above sea level. Its western and south-western parts have many volcanic rocks. Its population today is about 500,000. Madinah was also called Yathrab and Taibah.

Mosque of the Prophet

After Makkah, Madinah is the second most important city for all Muslims. It is Prophet Muhammad's (ⓓ) city where he took refuge to escape the persecution of the Quraish of Makkah. It is also the city of the Ansar (Prophet's Supporters). It is a city which loved the Prophet, and which he in turn loved most. On its soil he built his Holy Mosque (Masjid An-Nabi'). And it is in this city that he lies buried along with many of his early Companions.

The first important thing the Prophet did on arriving in Madinah was to build a mosque for prayer and as a meeting place. In fact, it was to serve as a community centre for all the religious, social and other activities of the Muslims. The land was bought from two orphans. The Prophet (ⓓ) himself carried stones like a labourer along with his companions. It was a simple building with a thatched roof and mud walls. This mosque came to be known as the Mosque of the Prophet (Masjid An-Nabi).

Brotherhood

The second important thing Muhammad (ⓓ) did in Madinah was to establish brotherhood between the emigrants from Makkah (Muhajirin) and the helpers of Madinah (Ansar) to solve the problem of refugees and displaced persons and to strengthen the ties of brotherhood between them. According to this Muslim brotherhood, the hosts were to share all their possessions with the emigrants, who had left everything in Makkah and were in great need of such help.

Thus the emigrants and their hosts were united into the bonds of brotherhood. Even the age-long enmity between the two tribes of Madinah, Aus and Khazraj, was forgotten.

Side view of Masjid An-Nabi (The Prophet's Mosque), Madinah.

Treaty with Jews

The next important step Muhammad (ﷺ) took to consolidate the position of Muslims in Madinah was to conclude a treaty with the neighbouring Jewish tribes for mutual help and defence of the city. This treaty achieved three main objectives:

Charter of liberty

It guaranteed freedom of thought and freedom of worship to the Muslims as well as the Jews. It also guaranteed protection of their lives and property. Peace and freedom to all the people, irrespective of colour or creed, was guaranteed and crime in all its forms was declared illegal. It secured freedom and equality for all citizens of Madinah.

Common Defence

This treaty was an attempt to establish friendly and cordial relations between the Muslims and the Jews of Madinah to live together as peaceful citizens and defend the town against invaders.

Leadership of the Prophet

This treaty also established the Prophet as the real leader and head of the state of Madinah. He was recognised as the controller of affairs; all disputes and other matters were to be referred to him. He was to act as an arbitrator between rival groups in case of quarrels and fights and maintain peace and order in the city state of Madinah.

The interior of the Prophet's Mosque, Madinah.

Organisation

After consolidation and establishment of Muslims in Madinah, the community was gradually organised on the basis of Divine Law. The affairs of the community concerning food, drink, marriage, trade and commerce, crime and punishment, war and peace, and social manners and morals were gradually brought under the Law of the Qur'an. Muhammad (ⓓ) was the undisputed leader, ruler, judge and commander of the people of Madinah.

Fasting

Fasting in the month of Ramadan was made obligatory upon all adult Muslims in the second year of Hijrah in these words of the Qur'an,

"O you who believe! Fasting is prescribed to you as it was prescribed to those before you, so that you may learn self-restraint." (2:183).

Dates, a traditional crop, continue to be an important product of Madinah.

Zakat

The payment of Zakat was also made obligatory upon all rich Muslims in the following words,

"And in their wealth and possessions is the right of the needy and of those who are deprived of the means of subsistence."(51:19).

Muslims are required to pay at least 2½ per cent of their savings at the end of the year.

Masjid al-Aqsa on the right and the Dome of the Rock on the left in this picture.

First Qibla in Jerusalem. Muslims praying in Jerusalem outside the mosque of Al Aqsa with the Dome of the Rock in view behind.

Change of Qiblah

As long as they lived in Makkah, Muhammad (ﷺ) and his followers used to pray facing the direction of the Mosque Al-Aqsa (of Jerusalem). When he came over to Madinah, he was ordered to pray in the direction of the Ka'bah. This was a clear indication that the era of the prophets of Israel had come to an end with the advent of Prophet Muhammad (ﷺ). It was therefore the right moment to establish the Ka'bah (at Makkah) as the religious centre for all Muslims.

Dome of Rock.

Ka'bah, the Qiblah of the Prophet Ibrahim

When the Prophet came to Madinah the situation was completely different. Here the Jews were in a strong and powerful position but had forsaken the way of life of the Prophet Ibrahim and adopted unjust and wrong ways of life. It was a clear signal of the end of the leadership of the Israelites. The following verse of the Qur'an declared this change of leadership and the new Spiritual Centre for mankind:

"So turn your face towards the Sacred Mosque (the Ka'bah). And wherever you are turn your faces towards it. And those who have been given the Book certainly know that it is the truth from their Lord." (The Qur'an: 2:144).

When this commandment was revealed the Prophet was leading the Dhuhr prayer in the house of Bishr-bin-Bara'-bin Ma'arur. He had gone through half of the prayer when this Commandment was revealed. He at once turned his face towards the Ka'bah during the prayer and all those who were offering their prayer with him did the same. Later on, it was announced publicly in Madinah and its suburbs that the Qiblah had been changed.

Hostility of the Quraish of Makkah

Peace is fundamental to life in Islam. And war comes only as a matter of necessity, when there is no other alternative course of action. The Qur'an clearly points out, "There has come to you, from Allah a Light and the Book, wherewith Allah guides all who seek His Pleasure to ways of peace and safety." (5:17-18). The Prophet Muhammad (ﷺ) invited people to this Light in a peaceful and friendly manner. His people opposed him and gradually this opposition became violent and fierce.

In spite of the opposition of the chiefs of Makkah, many virtuous, honest and truthful people accepted his call and embraced Islam. The chiefs of the Quraish were infuriated by his growing influence and intensified persecution and torture of the poor and weak converts to Islam. They even planned to kill him. The Prophet was then told to leave Makkah. Even in Madinah the Quraish chiefs did not let the Muslims live in peace for very long. They attacked Madinah three times but suffered humiliating defeats and then never dared to attack again. (For details of the battles please see chapter on Battles of the Prophet in this series of the author.)

A piece of calligraphy from the Prophet's Mosque, Madinah.

Treaty of Hudaibiyah

In the sixth year of Hijrah, Muhammad (D), with 1,400 companions, set out for Makkah for the pilgrimage of Umra. The Muslims camped at Hudaibiyah, a place just a few kilometres from Makkah in the direction of Jeddah. Muhammad (D) sent Othman to negotiate the terms of the pilgrimage with the chiefs of the Quraish, but he did not return and a rumour spread that he was killed. The Prophet (D) collected all his companions and took a pledge from them to sacrifice all, even their lives, if needed, in the cause of Islam. This is known as the Oath of Ridhwan (Bait-e-Ridhwan). This is mentioned in the Qur'an in these words,

"Allah's Good Pleasure was on the believers when they swore

The Well of Hudaibiyah. Probably the Prophet and his companions drank water from this well during their stay in the plain of Hudaibiyah. It is now filled with stones and rubbish and deserted.

Muhammad (ﷺ) entered Makkah as Commander of the Victorious army consisting of 10,000 Horsemen from the surrounding hills in the north east corner of this picture.

allegiance to you under the tree. He knew what was in their hearts and He sent down Peace to them, and rewarded them with a speedy victory." (48:18).

The Makkans threatened to stop Muslims by force of arms. The Prophet had come for the performance of Umra and wanted peace. So he accepted apparently an unfavourable peace of Hudaibiyah with the Command of Allah.

55

The Makkan leaders were disturbed when they heard of this and decided to negotiate a treaty of peace with Muhammad (☮). It was called the Treaty of Hudaibiyah and had the following terms:

1. The Muslims would return to Madinah that year.

2. They would come for the pilgrimage of Umra the following year but would stay for only three days in Makkah.

3. They would not take any Muslim from Makkah with them and would not stop any Muslim from staying in Makkah.

4. If any Makkan Muslim went to Madinah, they would return him to Makkah, but if any Muslim from Madinah went to Makkah he would not be returned to them.

5. The Quraish would neither attack the Muslims nor help others against them, but would remain neutral in case of Muslims fighting a third party.

These terms seemed very harsh and against the interests of the Muslims and naturally many of the Muslims, including 'Umar, felt bad about it. But the Prophet (☮) accepted it with the Command of Allah, and in the long run, it proved a blessing in disguise for the Muslim community.

The Makkan chiefs decided to negotiate a treaty of peace with the prophet. The treaty must have been signed somewhere in this plain of Hudaibiyah, around the village of Hudaibiyah.

Conquest of Makkah

The Treaty of Hudaibiyah gave the Muslims some peace and security and they had the opportunity to organise the Islamic state of Madinah. The Prophet even wrote letters to some rulers to the East and West inviting them to the Faith of Islam. But the peace was short-lived because the Treaty of Hudaibiyah was broken by the Chiefs of Makkah. Muhammad (ﷺ) very quietly marched on Makkah with an army of 10,000 Muslims on 10th of Ramadan in the eighth year of the Hijrah. The Makkans did not offer any resistance and the city of Makkah was captured without any fighting.

The Holy Mosque and the honourable Ka'bah 1884-5.

Makkan chiefs must have stood in this valley of Makkah, defeated and humiliated, on the other side of Ka'bah in this picture (on page 57). The Prophet announced a general pardon for all the enemies. He treated them all with affection and kindness. Only 3 or 4 persons who had committed grave offences of murder against innocent persons were executed.

Farewell Pilgrimage

With the conquest of Makkah, many people who had been waiting to see the result of the fighting between Muhammad (ⓓ) and the Quraish, were now fully convinced of the truthfulness of his Message and readily accepted Islam. Delegations from all over Arabia came to Madinah to embrace Islam. Thousands of people came into the fold of Islam after the conquest of Makkah.

The Prophet's mission was now completed and Islam spread to almost every home in the peninsula of Arabia. The Prophet made preparations for the Last Pilgrimage in the tenth year of Hijrah. In the plain of Arafat, near the Mount of Mercy (Jabal-e-Rehmah), he

The Mosque of Nimra in the Plain of Arafat.

delivered his Farewell Sermon to over 100,000 Muslims who had come from all over the country, for the pilgrimage.

The Prophet's Farewell Message

The Prophet delivered his last address to the people on the occasion of his Farewell Pilgrimage in the valley of Arafat (about nine miles from Makkah). His sermon was the climax of his twenty-three years of hard work and the fulfilment of his Mission. It was a message to mankind for all time.

The main points of the address were as follows:

1. Allah says, "O people! We created you from one male and one female and made you into tribes and nations, so that you may know each other. Indeed, in the Sight of Allah, the most honoured among you is the one who is most God-fearing." There is no superiority of an Arab over a non-Arab or of a non-Arab over an Arab, nor of

View of Arafat during the pilgrimage. The Muslims in hundreds of thousands gathered in the Plain of Arafat near Jabal-e-Rehmah to listen to the farewell message of the Prophet.

white over black nor black over white, except in Allah consciousness.

2. All mankind is the progeny of Adam; and Adam was created out of clay. Behold! Every claim of privilege, whether that of blood or property, is rejected.

3. Your blood, your property and your honour are sacred and inviolable until you appear before your Lord, as is this day of yours, this month of yours and this town of yours.

4. Indeed, you will soon meet your Lord and you will be held responsible for your actions.

5. You have certain rights over your women and they have certain rights over you. Treat them kindly, since they are your helpers.

6. All your debts must be repaid, all borrowed property must be returned, gifts should be reciprocated and guarantees must be honoured.

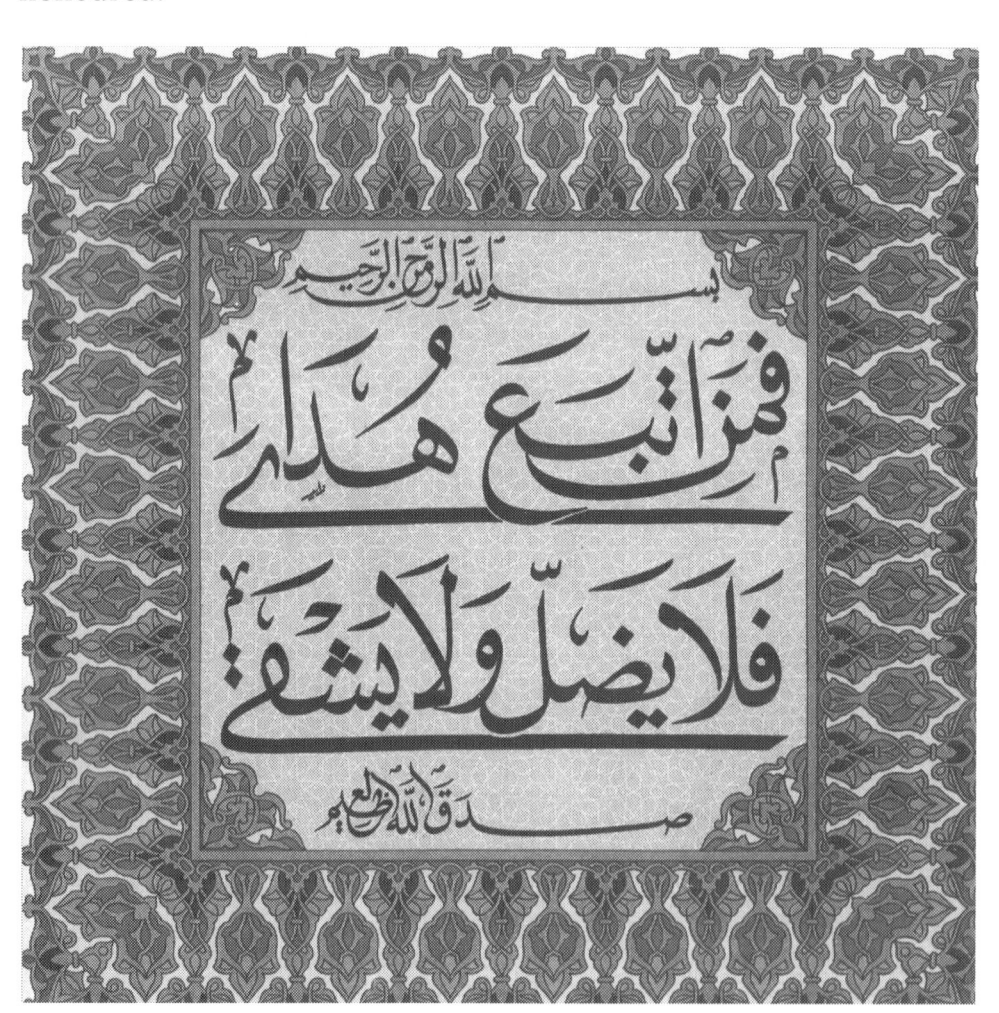

TRANSLATION: Then whosoever follows my guidance, will not go astray nor fall into misery. (The Qur'an: 20:123).

7. Everyone who commits a crime is himself responsible for it and no one else. A child is not responsible for the crime of his father, nor is the father responsible for the crime of his child.

8. It is not lawful for anyone to take anything of his brother's unless the latter gives it to him willingly.

9. Every Muslim is the brother of every other Muslim and all the Muslims form one brotherhood.

10. Feed and clothe your servants as well as you feed and clothe yourselves.

11. Listen to and obey your appointed ruler, even if he is a mangled Abyssinian slave, provided he executes the Law of Allah among you.

12. Beware of transgressing the limits set by Allah in matters of religion, for it was transgression which brought destruction to many peoples before you.

The Farewell Message of the Prophet (ⓓ) was delivered somewhere here on this side of Jabal-e-Rehmah where the car is parked.

In this sermon, The Prophet emphasised the importance of the Doctrine of Unity (Tawhid) and the coming of the Day of Judgement, and the sanctity of life, honour and property. He also emphasised the rights of women and the abolition of interest in Muslim societies. In the end, he told the Muslims that he was leaving the Book of Allah and the record of his own daily practice (Sunnah) with them. If they would hold fast to, and follow, these two things, they would never go wrong.

Jabal-e-Rehmah (mountain of Mercy) in the valley of Arafat. It is narrated that after their fall from the heaven, Adam and Eve, first met here in the Plain of Arafat.

The Prophet's Mosque after recent extension, with ten minarets, 1989-94.

Death

Two months after his return from the pilgrimage the Prophet (ﷺ) fell ill and died on Monday, 12th of Rabi-al-Awwal in the 11th year of Hijrah (the 23rd year of his Prophethood), June 633. May Allah's Peace and Blessing be upon him and upon his followers.

The Mission and Accomplishments of the Prophet Muhammad (ﷺ)

1. Prophet Muhammad (ﷺ) was, as the Qur'an says, sent by Allah as a mercy and blessing for mankind. His mission was to convey Allah's Way of Life to the people and he indeed accomplished this mission in his lifetime, as history shows.

2. He taught people the way to practise obedience to Allah, love for

mankind and justice in society by practising these virtues in his own personal life. It was in Madinah that he established this society and where he showed how justice could be practised in public life also.

3. It was Prophet Muhammad (ⒹⒹ) who introduced the concept of the Unity of Allah (Tawhid) and of the universe and showed its practical meaning in human life. It was no abstract myth, but a reality which was seen to pervade every detail of everyday life for all humanity.

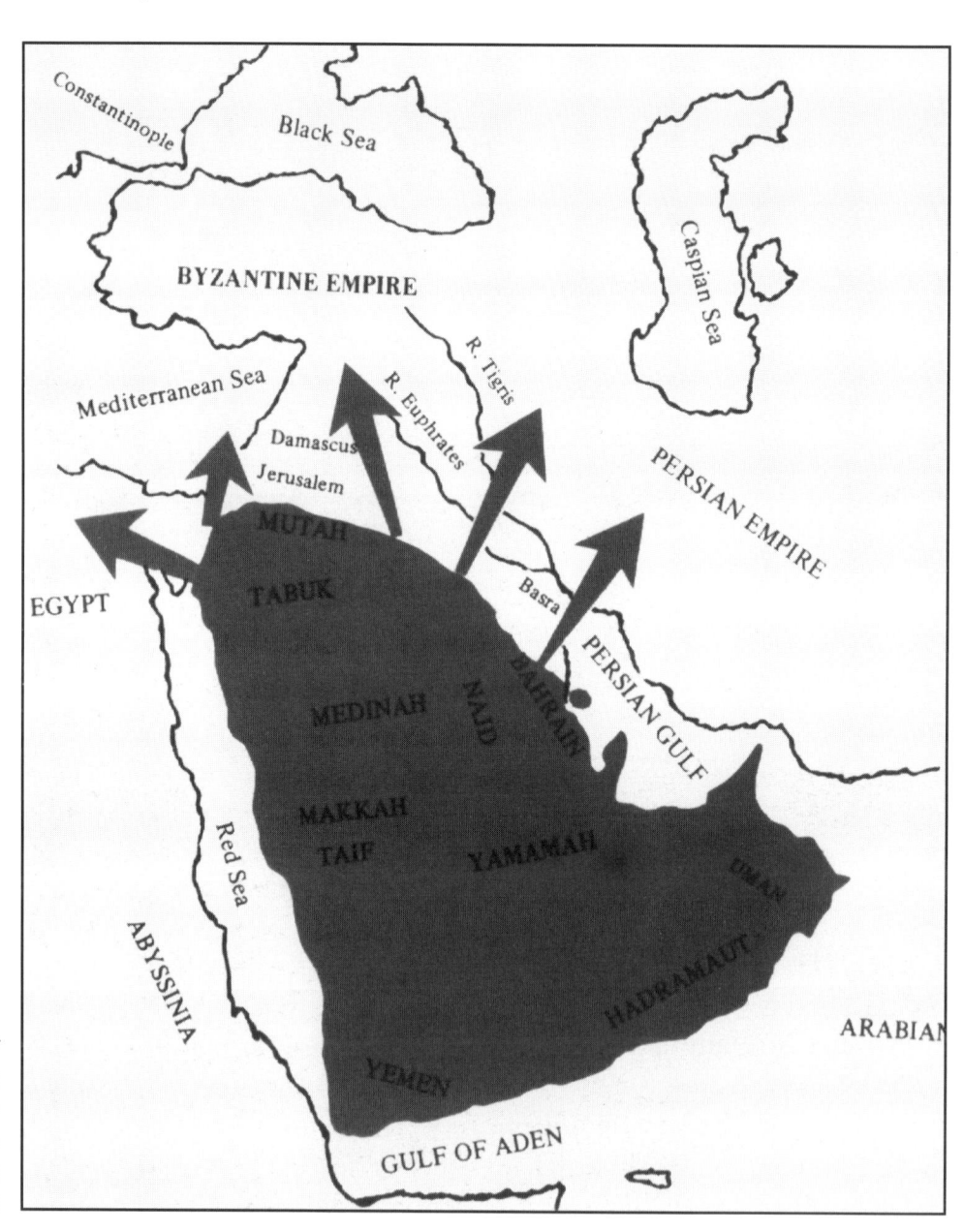

Political map of Arabia and neighbouring countries at the death of Muhammad (ⒹⒹ) (i.e., 532 C.E.)

4. He showed how the unity of Allah opened the way for the existence of a good and just system where everyone's rights were protected. This brought a complete change of society, which, in his time, was rife with tribal wars. The new faith demanded absolute equality of all members, without distinction of colour, race, tribe or sex. All were treated equally before Allah's Law in all spheres of life.
5. The rule of law was established and everyone was equal before law. Women were given equal rights with men and slaves were given equal status with other people.
6. The belief in the Unity of Allah also united spiritual and material aspects of life, showing that spiritual greatness and material progress

No sooner had the Prophet (ﷺ) emigrated from Makkah to Madinah in 622 G., he built a mosque with bricks and palm trees. When he passed away, he was buried where he died in the room of his wife, Eisha. The green dome in the middle shows the place of his burial in the Mosque of the Prophet, Madinah.

could go hand in hand. In fact, he pointed out, it was through the right use of material resources of life that one could attain spiritual excellence in the Sight of Allah. One's relationship with one's fellow men and women, whether family, neighbour or stranger, were all of a spiritual nature provided they were conducted in a way that would please Allah.

7. Brotherhood of man was the natural result of belief in One God (Allah). Brotherhood comprised not only those of the same society but included whole of mankind and worked for the good of all human beings.

8. Muhammad's (ⓓ) Message was meant for whole of mankind and created a society which was truly united under the spiritual law, although it contained people of different countries, nations, natures, dispositions and character. They all had the ideal of the oneness of the human race.

Another view of Prophet's Mosque.

9. The Prophet's universal religion, that is, Islam, which means submission to the Will of Allah, provided a foundation for the idea of a world community living in harmony, unity and peace, by obeying the Law of Allah.

10. The Prophet also showed man his real position in relation to the universe. He showed them how, by observing the physical world, they could see the Signs of Allah's Presence in everything and then by reflecting on these things, they would discover the secrets of Nature and gain control of the physical world, whose resources they would be able to use for the benefit of all mankind. (31:20). Thus he gave the secret of wealth and power to man. The acquisition of knowledge was to be the key to open the way to the treasures of

Side view of the Prophet's Mosque, Madinah.

Nature and the spirit of enquiry and reasoning would lead to success in all spheres of life.

11. It was the Prophet Muhammad (ﷺ) who led man to knowledge in place of ignorance, reason in place of superstitions and traditions, freedom of thought and research in place of blind acceptance of the opinions of ancestors and political leaders.

12. It was Muhammad (ﷺ) who brought man out of slavery both to other men and to his own ego and offered him the true mastery of his life in obedience to the Laws of Allah, his Creator.

Translation: And hold fast, all together, to the bond with Allah, and do not draw apart from one another. (Qur'an: 3:103).

واعتصموا بحبل الله جميعا ولا تفرقوا

Quality of his Life
Simple but High Living

Muhammad (ﷺ) lived a life of very high quality but his lifestyle was very simple and humble.

In his last years, he was the ruler of Arabia but he wore no crown, had no throne, lived in no palace, wore no costly dresses, had no guards and no army. He had no treasures of gold, silver and precious stones. He rarely had more than one pair of clothes which he washed himself. It is reported that at the last prayer he offered in public he was in one cloak. He was wearing the sheet over his shoulder on one side and under his armpit on the other.

The Word of Allah is always supreme.
(Holy Qur'an: 9:40).

His Residence

He lived in a small room with hardly any furniture in it. There were few things in it: A cot sewn with palm-tree strings and a leather pillow stuffed with palm-tree leaves. A leather bottle of water was hanging on the wall.

His Dress

Muhammad (D) lived a simple life. His simplicity was reflected in his dress, food and house. He disliked gaudy dresses of silk and dazzling colours and never wore a gold ring, much less precious stones. He liked white dress most of all, but sometimes wore clothes with a pale colour as well. Najashi, king of Abyssinia, sent him two pairs of socks of black colour as a present. He wore them and did dry ablution over them. He also wore shoes with two laces.

He would mend his own shoes and even patch his clothes. He combed his hair and wore a mantle to cover his body. In fact, he wore whatever was available. And He advised his rich followers, "If Allah shows His Favour to anyone, He likes the sign of His Bounty to be seen on His servant." And he also reported to have said, "Eat what you like and wear what you like so long as you avoid two things: extravagance and pride."

The house in which the Prophet was born and lived in Makkah is on the right in front of the block of buildings in this picture.

Refined Taste

Muhammad (☉) wore simple dress but was very neat and clean. He always liked cleanliness and refinement. He used perfumes and if anyone offered him a present of perfume he never rejected it.

Once he saw a man in dirty clothes, and said, "Can't he wash his clothes?" Once a man came to him wearing badly torn clothes. He said, "Have you any means (i.e., resources)?" He replied, "Yes." Muhammad (☉) said, "If Allah has given you His Blessing, it should be expressed through your appearance."

Once he saw a man with untidy hair and said, "Can't he put his hair in order?" Once people gathered in the mosque. As the mosque was narrow, and working people had come in dirty clothes, they sweated and the whole mosque was full of an unpleasant smell. The Prophet said, "It would have been better if you had taken a bath (before coming into the mosque)." From that same day, the Friday bath became an obligatory duty of the Muslims.

Meals

He never ate rich foods and delicacies all his life. When there was nothing to eat in the house, he would often fast. However, he liked honey, dates, olive oil, vinegar and of vegetables he liked the marrow. His food was simple, mostly barley bread and goat's milk.

Night view of the Prophet's Mosque, 1993.

He also liked a food called *hais* made of dates and cheese with butter. The Prophet liked vinegar as a seasoning in his food.

The food Allah's Messenger liked most was *tharid*. *Tharid* was a mixture of dates and butter and bread. In other words, bread mixed in a soup either of dates and butter or of meat.

Abu Hurairiah said that Allah's Messenger never expressed disapproval of food. If he desired it, he ate it. And if he disliked it, he left it alone.

His servant Anas said that he was not aware of Allah's Messenger having a thin loaf till he met Allah, nor did he ever see with his eyes a sheep roasted in its skin.

Allah's Messenger said, "Mention Allah's Name before eating, and eat with your right hand." It is reported that Allah's Messenger said, "Allah Most High is pleased when a person eats (or drinks) something and praises Him for it."

The Prophet also said: "The blessing of food consists in washing (hands) before it and washing after it."

The Prophet's Mosque in 1950.

Combing of Hair

Muhammad (ﷺ) combed his hair and did not like people to leave their hair flowing around in a dishevelled state. He also oiled his hair and combed his beard. His wife, A'isha, used to comb his hair.

White Hair

The Prophet Muhammad (ﷺ) was very healthy. He had hardly 18 or 20 white hair when he died.

The Prophet's Ring

The Prophet Muhammad (ﷺ) had a ring which he sometimes wore on his right hand and used it as his seal on official letters to kings, tribal chiefs and other dignitaries. It was made of silver and its stone was Ethiopian. But he did not always wear it.

The engraving on his ring was 'Muhammad Rasul Allah'. Allah was in the first line, Rasul in the second and Muhammad (ﷺ) in the third as below:

Allah

Rasul

Muhammad

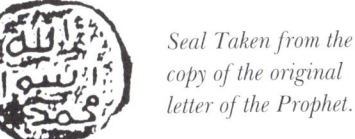

Seal Taken from the copy of the original letter of the Prophet.

(Impression of the Seal)

The Prophet's Sword

Prophet Muhammad (ⓓ) had several swords. Each of his swords had a proper name. The earliest sword that he inherited from his father was named *Mathoor*. His famous sword was named *Zulfiqar*. The knob of the hilt of this sword was made of silver. This sword was with the Prophet during the conquest of Makkah.

Coat of Armour

The Prophet had a few coats of armour. His famous coat of armour, named *Zat al Fuzool*, was pawned with a Jew when he died.

It is reported that he had two coats of armour on him in the battle of Uhud.

Helmet

When the Prophet entered Makkah on the Day of the victory, he had a helmet on his head. He had also a helmet on his head in the battle of Uhud.

Early mosque, Khaybar. Minaret from the north.

The Prophet's Oratory

Eloquence was highly rated among the Arabs. Muhammad (ﷺ) enjoyed an Allah-given gift of eloquence and he knew the value of eloquence. Once he said, "I am the most eloquent of the Arabs. I am raised with comprehensive words."

He was brought up in the Tribe of Banu Hawazin and born in the Tribe of the Quraish. These two tribes of Arabia had a special distinction in the art of eloquence and oratory. The Prophet also said, "I am the most eloquent of you; I am Quraishi and my language is of Banu Sa'd, (a branch of Banu Hawazin)."

The Prophet spoke in a simple but very effective way. His Farewell Address on his Last Pilgrimage is a masterpiece of simplicity and beauty of expression. (Please see his Farewell Address in this series.)

A view of Jabal-e-Rehmah in Arafat.

Conversation

The Prophet Muhammad (ﷺ) talked softly, neither too slow nor fast but in a friendly and endearing manner. The listeners could easily understand him and remember what he said. His wife, A'isha Siddiqah said, "Allah's Messenger did not go on talking rapidly as you do, but would talk in such a way that anyone who wished to count his words would be able to do so." A Companion of the Prophet said, "Allah's Messenger spoke in a distinct and relaxed manner."

Regarding his manners, it is reported that when he shook hands with anyone he did not withdraw his hand till the other did so. When talking to someone he did not turn his face away till the other did so. And he was never seen to put forward his knees in front of one with whom he was sitting.

Details of artistic designs on the pillars in the Prophet's Mosque, Madinah.

Assemblies

Everybody was welcome to his meetings, where he talked to people as a wise and sympathetic friend. Bedouins would often come in their own crude manner and ask him questions boldly. The prophet sat with his Companions without any distinction. The newcomer had often to ask, "Who amongst you is Muhammad?" The Companions then informed them which one was the Prophet of Allah.

Bedouins would often say, "O Ibn Abd al Muttalib! I will ask you

Side view of the Prophet's Mosque.

questions very harshly, but don't be angry!" The Prophet would willingly allow them to ask questions.

In spite of this simplicity and humility, the assembly of the Prophet was full of dignity and decorum of the Prophethood. And talk was mostly confined to religion, morals and things which were likely to improve, or purify, people's lives, morals and character. However, sometimes people indulged in asking about the very common things of life.

He always delivered very short sermons. His longest address is his Farewell Address which he delivered in the plain of Arafat at the time of his Farewell Pilgrimage. And this is about a thirty minute talk.

Daily Routine

The Prophet Muhammad (ⓓ) divided his time into three parts; one for worship (i.e., ibadah), a second for people, and a third for his own person.

It was his usual custom to sit down after the morning prayer till the sun was well up. This was the time for public assembly. People would come and sit around him. He would say to them a few words of advice. Then they would talk about general things relating to the affairs of life.

Inside view of the gates of the Prophet's Mosque.

In mid morning he offered short prayers and then got busy in household work. He offered the noon (zuhr) prayers and retired for siesta. Activity began after Asr prayer. He called at the dwellings of his wives one by one. Then he stayed back with the one whose turn it was that night.

In the evening, all the wives would go there and stay till the night prayer. Then he would go to the mosque to offer his night (i'sha) prayer and thereafter go to sleep. All the other wives would go to their own houses. He did not like conversation after the night prayer.

Night Worship

Before going to bed he recited some Surah of the Qur'an and slept in the first part of the night after i'sha prayer.

He got up after midnight or when one-third of the night was left. First he would clean his teeth with his tooth stick (miswak), wash himself (ablution) and then engage himself in prayers in the deep silence of the night.

He always slept on his right side with his right hand under his cheek. He also snored a little in his sleep.

There was no special bedding for him. Sometimes he slept on an ordinary bed, sometimes on the skin, and sometimes he rested on the bare floor.

Inside view of the Prophet's Mosque.

Practice on Journeys

He undertook travel for different reasons. Firstly it was for trade, then mostly for jihad. His usual practice was that he cast a lot among his wives. And she whose name was drawn would go with him on that journey.

He often started early in the morning. When he put his foot in the stirrup, he said, "In the name of Allah (Bism il lah)." When he got in the saddle, he said takbir (i.e., Allah O Akbar), three times. Then he recited this verse, "Glory be to Him who made this animal tame for us, we could not have made it submit to us. And we are all to return to our Lord." (The Qur'an: 43:13–14).

The Prophet's Mosque. A general view from inside.

Muhammad (ﷺ) The Perfect Man His Morals and Practice

It is the privilege of Prophet Muhammad (ﷺ) alone of all reformers, philosophers and founders of religions, to bequeath to his successors a complete and perfect life-example — a life-example capable of solving all their problems, and purifying their words and deeds, hearts and souls, morals and manners, civilisation and culture.

His lifestyle is not only perfect but fully comprehensive. It covers every aspect and every field of human activity. It offers guidance to all men and women in every area of their lives to solve their problems fairly and justly. Its principles and concepts are simple and easily understandable to all people of all abilities. And it offers them true satisfaction and peace in meeting their material desires as well as reaching spiritual excellence.

He has given us simple recipe to solve our multifarious problems easily and attain real and lasting peace and happiness.

The Prophet Muhammad (ﷺ) gave lessons on morality and manners through his practice. He taught charity by distributing everything that he received among the poor and the needy. He taught love and forgiveness to his enemies as conqueror of Makkah and Hunain. He taught justice and equity as ruler and judge. He demonstrated his desire of peace and security to his enemies as commander of the victorious army. He taught fairness in dealing with other people by his practice as a trader. And he gave lessons on love, affection and kindness as a husband and father.

All these morals and virtues he practised and, thereby, invited all members of humanity to enrich themselves materially, morally and spiritually by following in his footprints.

It seems realistic that only a man like Muhammad (ﷺ), of flesh and blood, who lived like ordinary human beings, but rose far above them in the conduct of his affairs (a) with his family members and (b) other people in different areas of life, can truly serve as a good and practical example for mankind.

Muhammad (D) led a simple but very virtuous life. He was married and had children. As a married man, he has left unique principles of human relations (D) between a husband and his wife and (b) between a father and his children.

Professionally he was a trader. And in business transactions and the economic field he has given unparalleled ideas and principles: principles to establish a balanced and exemplary economic system for the benefit of mankind.

TRANSLATION: *And surely Muhammad (D) you are exalted to a sublime and noble character.*
(The Qur'an: 68:4).

He was required to make certain laws for meeting the needs of his people. But in this process of law-making, he has given a lead to mankind in the philosophy, principles and wisdom of law. He has laid down fair and just rules and regulations for guiding the processes of legislation.

As a judge, he has demonstrated the significance and importance of the rule of law and impartiality (a) in applying law to specific cases, (b) in judging between various people in their mutual disputes, and (c) as well as disputes between them and other peoples.

TRANSLATION: *In the name of Allah, Compassionate, Merciful. Indeed a Messenger has come to you from among yourselves. It grieves him that you should perish: he is greedily anxious for your true success: he is most kind and compassionate to the believers.*
(The Qur'an: 9:128).

Muhammad (ﷺ) did not regard himself as a superman or a godhead, but just a man like any other man, working for a living and leading a normal life. However, there was this difference between him and other people that he received Divine Guidance, in the Light of which his word and action received perfection. Thus it provided a perfect example for mankind in every area of human activity.

A person whose complete lifestyle and life-example is preserved, who lived a full term in the hustle and bustle of life and whose activities in full detail are clear and open, can really serve as a perfect model and ideal for guiding the lives of all members of humanity.

Another essential ingredient of a perfect lifestyle is universality and completeness. In other words, the lifestyle must cover every aspect of human existence. It must cater for the needs and demands of people of all abilities, capacities, temperaments and inclinations, materially as well as spiritually.

The third essential ingredient of a perfect lifestyle is practicality. We have to see how far the principles, teachings and concepts of a person were observed in practice. And how successfully did they solve the problems of the people in their practical lives. This is because mere verbal ideology and philosophy of life without any roots in human practical life are not enough.

It is obvious that a perfect lifestyle cannot truly be measured in terms of sermons and high moral principles. It can only be measured by practical achievements in life. And simple high ideals cannot become guidelines for people unless they are supported by practical deeds.

TRANSLATION: In the name of Allah, Most Gracious, Most Merciful. (The Qur'an: 1:1).

How can anyone set an example of forgiveness towards enemies without gaining victory over them?

How can anyone set an example of generosity towards the poor and the destitute while living a lonely life in solitude?

How can anyone advise on matrimonial problems who did not experience married life?

How can anyone make rules and principles for the businessman, judge, ruler and commander etc., without himself experiencing certain problems in these situations?

How can anyone deliver sermons on love and affection for the sick and invalids, without having himself done it?

Obviously, only a person who has lived through all these situations and gained first hand experience is in a position to set guidelines for others. There is no man in history who has been put to test in all these situations in life and who has come out successfully and given concepts and principles governing human relationships which he himself experienced and practised except for Prophet Muhammad (Ⓓ).

TRANSLATION:
Grieve not, truly, Allah is with us.
(The Qur'an: 9:40).

Thus to look for a lifestyle that is perfect and ideal as a guide for the whole of mankind, we must find in it authenticity, perfection, completeness and practicality.

Although it is true that all the prophets of Allah were perfect guides for mankind, yet their teachings and life-histories have been lost, so that now only brief, sketchy and fragmented events of their lives are known. And even these are not historically reliable.

Therefore, as the records stand, their lives and teachings can hardly be presented as perfect and ideal examples for mankind.

On the other hand, the teachings and lifestyle of Prophet Muhammad (ⒹⒹ) stand as perfect and ideal today as they did 1400 years ago, without any change or alteration.

TRANSLATION: And we have not sent you but as a mercy to the nations. (The Qur'an: 21:107).

If we judge the lifestyle of Muhammad (ⒹⒹ) on the basis of reliability, we find that there is a universal agreement by historians that the record of the life and teachings of the Prophet (ⒹⒹ) has been very carefully preserved by his followers.

This fact is confirmed even by the opponents of Islam. Dr. Sprenger, a German writer, says, "There is no nation, nor has there been any, which like them, has, during twelve centuries, recorded the life of every man of letters."

And John Devonport writes, "Of all law-makers and conquerors, there is none the events of whose life are more true and detailed than those of Prophet Muhammad (ⒹⒹ)."

Every word and every act of Prophet Muhammad (ⒹⒹ) has been recorded. His whole life, with details of movements and actions from birth to death are fully recorded and preserved. His family-life with his wives and children, his prayers, his conduct at home and with his followers, his business transactions, his preaching to the people, and all the opposition and wars with them, are fully recorded and preserved.

Even the features of his physical person, his way of speaking, walking, talking, standing, etc., is recorded. As Gibbon says, "No Prophet tested his disciples in such fiery ideals as Muhammad (ⒹⒹ), the Prophet, did. He preached the Divine Mission and declared himself a Prophet to those who knew him as a man, to his wife, servant, and intimate friends. They all believed in him and embraced his faith."

Nothing of his life was kept hidden from the public. It was an open book for everyone to observe. He had even permitted his wives to reveal his private life to the people. The details of his morals, manners and way of life are completely recorded.

He has left treasures of instructions by his word and deed on every aspect of human life, from spiritual and moral to economic and political. In fact, all problems of man from the cradle to the grave are completely covered in his life-style.

The picture of his life-style is so richly and vividly described in the historical records that one feels as if one is actually watching the Prophet engaged in his daily work and talking to his wives and addressing people in the Mosque after prayer.

١٠٨- قُلْ يَا أَيُّهَا النَّاسُ قَدْ جَاءَكُمُ الْحَقُّ مِنْ رَبِّكُمْ فَمَنِ اهْتَدَىٰ فَإِنَّمَا يَهْتَدِي لِنَفْسِهِ وَمَنْ ضَلَّ فَإِنَّمَا يَضِلُّ عَلَيْهَا وَمَا أَنَا عَلَيْكُمْ بِوَكِيلٍ ۞

TRANSLATION: Say O People! The Truth has indeed come to you from your Lord! Those who receive guidance, do so for the good of their own souls; those who astray, do so to their own loss, and I am not a custodian over you. (The Qur'an: 10:108).

There is no example in history where so many people were willingly prepared to sacrifice their lives and everything for the sake of one man. They must have seen him, observed him and tested him from every angle, and then found him absolutely perfect in every way; otherwise they would not have so readily sacrificed their lives of their own accord.

All these are concrete facts of his life, not mere fanciful stories or abstract virtues and mere concepts.

Thus it seems, in the presence of the complete and perfect life of Muhammad (ⓓ), the purity and nobility of his thoughts and perfection of his morals and manners, there is no place for any other guide.

Above all, his thoughts, concepts and principles were fully tested in the furnace of practicability. His character and conduct was fully put to test in his life at Makkah and then at Madinah. He passed through varying situations of extreme persecution and oppression at Makkah; then after wars and open hostilities with the chiefs of

Makkah and the rest of the country with his ultimate triumph over all his enemies. During these many years of trial, he showed no signs of pessimism or frustration at the former or of pride and boastfulness at the latter.

The nobility and greatness of his character is fully borne out by his actions and practices at home with his family and outside among his Companions and other people.

للرِّجَالِ نَصِيبٌ مِمَّا تَرَكَ الْوَالِدَانِ وَالْأَقْرَبُونَ وَلِلنِّسَاءِ نَصِيبٌ مِمَّا تَرَكَ الْوَالِدَانِ وَالْأَقْرَبُونَ مِمَّا قَلَّ مِنْهُ أَوْ كَثُرَ نَصِيبًا مَفْرُوضًا

TRANSLATION:
For men is a share of what the parents and near relatives leave, and for women a share of what the parents and the near relatives leave, whether it be little or much - an appointed share. (The Qur'an: 4:7).

His conduct as a husband, father, trader, judge and in any other capacity fully confirms the principles and manners given by him in these fields of life. Likewise, his code of conduct for a ruler, educator, military leader, administrator, or statesman, is fully supported by his practice in these positions.

There is absolutely no difference in his words and actions, and moral precepts and practices in life. Everything he said, he proved it by his own practice. And he condemned those people who preach to others what they do not practise themselves. (Qur'an: 61:2).

The Qur'an is the Divine Book of Guidance. And Muhammad (ⓓ) is seen as the Divine Book in practice, for he never preached and told anything to the people which he did not himself practise. He was, in fact, the Qur'an in practice. Once someone asked his wife A'isha about the morals of the Prophet. She replied, "The Qur'an is his morals." What she meant was that he did not tell people to do anything unless he himself first practised it.

Muhammad (ⓓ) was indeed the Qur'an in practice: the perfect specimen of man created in the image of Allah.

Kalimah: The Article of Faith: There is no god but Allah. Muhammad is the Messenger of Allah.

The Key to Muhammad's (D) Perfection is Constancy in Conduct

It is a great virtue that one should adopt good morals and then practise them constantly in such a way that it becomes a habit. Muhammad (D) very strictly observed this principle in his life. Whatever rules and regulations he set in the Light of Divine Guidance, he always practised them in his life. No change was ever observed in his normal standards of conduct throughout his life.

Once someone asked A'isha about his ways and deeds of worship. She replied, "His action was like a shower from the clouds. Just as when a shower falls it does not stop, likewise, when the Prophet adopted anything, he always observed it regularly."

This is why the Prophet said, "The most loved deed in the Sight of Allah is the one which a person does perpetually." He never changed any of his conduct or practice. And his practice (i.e., Sunnah) is now the Code of Conduct in all matters for the Muslims.

وَقُلْ اٰمَنْتُ بِمَآ اَنْزَلَ اللّٰهُ مِنْ كِتٰبٍ وَاُمِرْتُ لِاَعْدِلَ بَيْنَكُمْ ۚ اَللّٰهُ رَبُّنَا وَرَبُّكُمْ ۚ لَنَآ اَعْمَالُنَا وَلَكُمْ اَعْمَالُكُمْ ۚ لَا حُجَّةَ بَيْنَنَا وَبَيْنَكُمْ ۚ اَللّٰهُ يَجْمَعُ بَيْنَنَا ۚ وَاِلَيْهِ الْمَصِيْرُ ۚ

TRANSLATION: Say: I believe in what Allah has revealed of the book, and I am commanded to do justice between you. Allah is our Lord and your Lord. For us are our deeds; and for you your deeds. There is no contention between us and you. Allah will gather us together and to Him is our final goal. (The Qur'an: 42:15).

Grave of Prophet Muhammad (ﷺ) in Masjid-e-Nabi.

Behind the door his grave is completely covered by a curtain and is not visible to anyone who peeps through the holes of the wall. He will see only the curtain.

Charming and Elegant Manners

Muhammad (ﷺ) was an embodiment of excellent morals and character. And his graceful conduct and charming manners daily demonstrated the perfection of his noble character.

He taught good moral principles to people and himself practised what he preached. He was indeed an excellent example for all mankind in his conduct and manners. The Qur'an mentions the nobility and sublimity of his character in these words: "You indeed stand on an exalted standard of character." (68:4).

It is reported by many eminent Companions that the Prophet was most polite, courteous and gentle in manners. He talked with grace and dignity and his face was always smiling. He never hurt anyone's heart or feelings. His servant Anas said that the Prophet was the best of men in character. Many of his Companions also reported that they had seen no one more given to smiling than Allah's Messenger.

It was his practice that in meeting people he greeted and shook hands with them first. When walking on the way he greeted all men, women, and children whoever came before him. In assemblies, undesirable incidents happened but he tolerated them all and never said anything to anyone.

Fair Dealing

He was very fair and just in his business dealings with other people, and there was never any complaint of any kind against him. All those people with whom he had business dealings before

Prophethood always praised his honest and fair dealing. The people of Makkah therefore called him the Truthful (sadiq) and Trustworthy (Amin).

Once a Bedouin came to claim his debt from the Prophet. He began to talk to the Prophet very harshly. The Companions reprimanded him on his arrogant behaviour and said to him, "Do you know with whom you are talking?" He said he was demanding his right.

The Prophet told his Companions that they should be with him for it was his right (to claim his debt). Then he asked the Companions to pay off his debt and some more.

Once he bought a camel and paid off the debt with a better camel, saying, "The best of people are those who pay off their debt nicely."

TRANSLATION: Truly Allah commands you to make over trusts to those worthy of them, and that when you judge between people, you judge with justice. Truly how excellent is the teaching which He gives you! For Allah is He who hears and sees all things. (The Qur'an: 4:58).

Once he bought some dates from a man. The man came after a few days to claim his dates. The Prophet asked one of his Companions to pay off his debt. The Companions paid him dates which were not of the same quality as he had given. He refused to accept them. The companions asked him whether he was refusing to accept dates given by Allah's Messenger.

The man said, "If Allah's Messenger does not do justice, then from whom should we hope for it?" The Prophet heard these words and tears came into his eyes, and said, "He is quite right." (Then the man was given dates of the same quality and some more.)

The Prophet borrowed some armour from an unbeliever in the battle of Hunain with the promise to pay compensation if any of these were lost. When returning the Prophet said to the lender, "A few suits of armour are missing; accept compensation for them." The unbeliever replied, "O Allah's Messenger! The condition of my heart is not as it was before! In other words, I have accepted Islam. Now I don't need any compensation." (These incidents are of the time when Muhammad (ﷺ) was the ruler of the state of Madinah.)

His Lifestyle

There is no doubt that only the right type of action, like the right type of trade, can prosper and succeed. Others cannot compete for long. It is the right conduct and true words that are the only key to happiness and peace, in the physical as well as the spiritual sense.

Evil conduct and wrongdoing may seem to flourish for a while but it can never prosper in the long run.

The Qur'an presents a simple and truthful life of Muhammad (ﷺ) to the people to judge, understand and follow if they want real prosperity, success and peace in life. It stresses: "I have already lived a lifetime among you before revelation. will you not then understand?" (The Qur'an:10:16).

وَأَوْفُوا الْكَيْلَ وَالْمِيزَانَ بِالْقِسْطِ
لَا نُكَلِّفُ نَفْسًا إِلَّا وُسْعَهَا
وَإِذَا قُلْتُمْ فَاعْدِلُوا
وَلَوْ كَانَ ذَا قُرْبَىٰ
وَبِعَهْدِ اللَّهِ أَوْفُوا
ذَٰلِكُمْ وَصَّاكُم بِهِ لَعَلَّكُمْ تَذَكَّرُونَ

TRANSLATION: And give full measure and weight with equity – We impose not on any soul a duty but to the extent of its ability. And when you speak, speak justly, even if a relative is concerned. And fulfil Allah's Covenant. Thus does he command you, that you may remember.
(The Qur'an: 6:152).

The argument of this verse of the Qur'an is this: You have witnessed forty years of his life before the revelation of the Qur'an. And you know that Muhammad (ﷺ) never told a single lie or practised any kind of deceit or cunning all his life. And all those people with whom he had come into contact in any capacity bore witness to the fact that he had been truthful, honest and trustworthy.

Prophet Muhammad (ﷺ) is thus asked to remind his people: "I am not a stranger among you. I have lived a life-time of forty years among you before this revelation of the Qur'an. How can you expect from my past that I would present the Qur'an to you, as Allah's Book, without gaining knowledge from Him and without His Command? A man who had never told a lie in the worldly affairs, how could he tell a lie about Allah?"

وَمَا أَرْسَلْنَاكَ إِلَّا رَحْمَةً لِّلْعَالَمِينَ

TRANSLATION: And we have not sent you but as a mercy to the nations.
(The Qur'an: 21:107).

The people of Makkah knew well what kind of life Muhammad (ﷺ) was leading till a day before the revelation. They were fully aware of his occupation, of the topics of his conversation, of the nature of his interests and activities. No doubt it was a life which was an embodiment of truth, honesty and justice – a model of nobility, peacefulness, fulfilment of obligations to others and of service of humanity.

There was nothing in it which could give anybody any idea that Muhammad (ﷺ) was going to make a claim to Prophethood the next day. He had never stood up to preach, had never started a movement of any kind; and none of his activities had ever indicated that he was anxious to undertake any programme for religious or moral reformation.

وَأَنفِقُوا۟ فِى سَبِيلِ ٱللَّهِ وَلَا تُلْقُوا۟ بِأَيْدِيكُمْ إِلَى ٱلتَّهْلُكَةِ ۛ وَأَحْسِنُوٓا۟ ۛ إِنَّ ٱللَّهَ يُحِبُّ ٱلْمُحْسِنِينَ ۝

TRANSLATION: And give (your wealth) in charity in the Way of Allah, and make not your own hands contribute to (your) destruction; but do good, for Allah loves those who do good (to others). (The Qur'an: 2:195).

All these things were clear and openly known to the people of Makkah. When the sincere and honest people of Makkah heard such verses of the Qur'an they believed in him.

Naturally the pure and virtuous life of Prophet Muhammad (ﷺ) had an amazing and miraculous effect on the lives of the sincere and truth-loving people of Makkah and the surrounding areas. It was very hard for them to doubt the truthfulness of his Message and Revelation of Allah.

The Perfect Human Being

Muhammad (ﷺ) was human, made of flesh and blood, like any other human being. But he was a perfect human in every sense and set a code of conduct by his words and actions. It is unique and unparalleled in human history and will remain a guide for other men and women in every aspect of life for ever.

He left a way of life that surpasses all other ideas and

philosophies of life. It gives mankind a balanced view of everything.

It treats man (and woman) as normal human beings with desires and weaknesses. But shows them a way to satisfy their desires, as well as overpower their weaknesses – a way by which they can rise higher in status than even the Angels in spirituality, yet at the same time remain humble and pious creatures of the earth.

وَإِنْ عَاقَبْتُمْ فَعَاقِبُوْا بِمِثْلِ مَا عُوْقِبْتُمْ بِهِ ۖ وَلَئِنْ صَبَرْتُمْ لَهُوَ خَيْرٌ لِلصَّابِرِيْنَ ۝

TRANSLATION: And if you retaliate, let your retaliation be to the extent that with which you were afflicted. But if you show patience, it is indeed best for those who are patient.
(The Qur'an:16:126).

This was what made Muhammad (ⒹⒷ) perfect and excel all other human beings. He neither asked them to leave the worldly life and live in isolation, engaged all the time in worship and meditation, nor advised them to indulge all the time in the pursuits of the material world. Muhammad (ⒹⒷ) gave an entirely new philosophy of life to mankind: that they may continue living a normal life but (a) believe in the Lordship and Sovereignty of Allah and (b) strive to obey and follow His Code of Law and (c) they should always keep in mind, while engaged in their normal work, that they are servants of Allah; and, as such, they have to obey and follow His Commands.

لَا تَعْبُدُوْنَ إِلَّا اللهَ ۙ وَبِالْوَالِدَيْنِ إِحْسَانًا وَذِى الْقُرْبٰى وَالْيَتٰمٰى وَالْمَسٰكِيْنِ وَقُوْلُوْا لِلنَّاسِ حُسْنًا وَ

TRANSLATION: You shall serve none but Allah. And do good to (your) parents, to your relatives, to the orphans and to the needy, and speak to all people in a kindly way.
(The Qur'an:2:83).

At home, while living with the family, they should see that nothing is done that is against the Command of Allah.

In business, they should see that they do not earn the Displeasure of Allah by fraud, cheating or doing unlawful things in dealing with others.

In service, they should see that (a) no decision is taken against the clear Commandments of Allah and His Messenger, and (b) no injustice is done to anyone.

In the capacity of a ruler or a judge, they shoud see that absolute justice is done to all.

In short, it is the duty of every citizen of the Islamic state to see and ensure that Way of Allah and His Messenger is established in totality; covering all areas and departments of human activity.

لِلَّذِينَ اَحْسَنُوا الْحُسْنٰى وَزِيَادَةٌ ۚ

TRANSLATION:
Those who do good (to others) will get good reward and even more than their merits.
(The Qur'an:10:26).

This attitude of life would bring peace, happiness and justice to every home. All petty disputes would disappear, because all would obey one law, i.e., the Law of Allah and His Messenger. According to this philosophy of life, (a) working to earn an honest living in any profession, (b) feeding one's family, (c) respecting elders and showing affection to younger ones, (d) helping in family's work at home, (e) removing any harmful and dangerous thing from the road (or footpath) likely to cause damage or injury to anyone; and (f) even satisfaction of one's sexual desire with one's wife, is a charity (and, as such, an act of piety and virtue).

This shows that every act of normal working of a man (or woman) becomes an act of piety and goodness if it is done in obedience to the Command of Allah and His Messenger. And, by doing this work sincerely and wholeheartedly in the service of the Sovereign, man (or woman) rises to the highest station of excellence in the domain of morality and spirituality.

Here lies the greatness and excellence of Prophet Muhammad (ﷺ). He gave ordinary men and women an opportunity to attain the highest possible station in Nearness to Allah while enjoying their normal lives at home and at work. Muhammad (ﷺ) attained this status himself and then invited other people to achieve this noble goal.

The conduct, behaviour and way of life of Prophet Muhammad (ﷺ) is exemplary in every way for humanity. In fact, it is the final and most excellent specimen of human conduct and behaviour available to mankind. It is commendable that all human beings should endeavour to aspire to and copy his conduct and behaviour. This is the only way in which they can rightly steer their lives with success and happiness to their final destination; individually as well as collectively.

In fact, "now the only means to achieve success, excellence and peace, in the worldly as well as spiritual life, is to follow the life-style of Prophet Muhammad (ﷺ)." He has left a complete and perfect system of thought, practice and civilisation. And has given detailed principles for the solution of multifarious human problems. His Guidance is, therefore, the only relevant way of life for modern man to solve his complex and complicated personal and social problems.

إِنْ أَحْسَنتُمْ أَحْسَنتُمْ لِأَنفُسِكُمْ وَإِنْ أَسَأْتُمْ فَلَهَا

TRANSLATION:
If you do good, you do good for yourselves. And if you do evil, you do it against yourselves.
(The Qur'an:17:7).

Moral Perfection

The real purpose of Prophet Muhammad (ﷺ) was to improve morals of the people. Muhammad (ﷺ) explained this in these words, "I am sent to perfect morals and good conduct." He always kept this object before him.

According to his wife A'isha, the Prophet used to pray: "O Allah! as You have made my form beautiful, so make my character beautiful." And it is also reported that he said, "The believers whose faith is most perfect are those who have the best character."

وَتَعَاوَنُوا۟ عَلَى ٱلْبِرِّ وَٱلتَّقْوَىٰ وَلَا تَعَاوَنُوا۟ عَلَى ٱلْإِثْمِ وَٱلْعُدْوَٰنِ وَٱتَّقُوا۟ ٱللَّهَ إِنَّ ٱللَّهَ شَدِيدُ ٱلْعِقَابِ

TRANSLATION: And help one another in righteousness and piety, and help not one another in sin and aggression, and keep your duty to Allah.
(The Qur'an: 5:2).

This book is finished in all Humility to Allah the Almighty and Mercy and Blessings to our Prophet.

Peace be upon him.

OTHER PUBLICATIONS
BY THE AUTHOR
1. Muhammad Encyclopaedia of Seerah
   Vols I to VIII   (HB)   £240.00
   Each volume   (HB)   £30.00
2. Prayer, its significance and Benefits
   302 pages   (PB)   £5.00
3. Islam, Ideology and Way of Life,
   409 pages   (PB)   £5.00
4. Muhammad Blessing for Mankind
   337 pages   (PB)   £5.00
5. Role of Muslim Women in Society
   450 pages   (PB)   £8.90
6. Seerah Series
   Readings in Islamic Political Philosophy
   330 pages Vol. I Liberty   (PB)   £8.90
7. Islam: Faith and Practice for High School Students.
   (with pictures and illustrations)
   234 pages   (PB)   £4.20

AUTHOR: AFZALUR RAHMAN
ADVANCE PAYMENT: All cheques and bankdrafts in favour of Seerah Foundation, 78 Gillespie Road, London N5 1LN. Plus postage.
Discount for booksellers – 33% (UK) and 40% (Overseas)
Tel. office: 071-359 8257 Residence: 071-359 0373.